THE POLITICS OF LOVE:

The New Testament and Nonviolent Revolution

THE POLITICS OF LOVE:

The New Testament and Nonviolent Revolution

by

JOHN FERGUSON

FELLOWSHIP PUBLICATIONS
Nyack, New York
1979

For Jack and Bunty

Published by the Fellowship of Reconciliation
Box 271, Nyack, New York 10960

Copyright ©1977 by Fellowship of Reconciliation
New Malden, Surrey, England
American edition published by arrangement
with James Clarke & Co., Ltd., Cambridge, England

Printed in the United States of America
Library of Congress Catalog Card Number: 79-16508
International Standard Book Number: 0-911810-08-0

CONTENTS

CONTENTS

PROLOGUE

In 1936 Professor G.H.C. Macgregor wrote his well-known book *The New Testament Basis of Pacifism*. It has been reprinted many times and has helped innumerable people to a fuller understanding of this aspect of the witness of the New Testament. As stocks of the latest edition became exhausted there was a question whether to issue a new reprint. The basic problem can be easily put. First, the general approach to biblical studies has moved and scholars are not greatly interested in the manipulation of isolated texts. On the other hand it is the experience of those who speak in public that these texts do still exercise their audience; there are questions which need to be answered. Second, Macgregor's superbly scholarly book was in other ways too a book of the thirties: it uses the Revised Version of the Bible: it makes constant reference to the controversies of the thirties. A full reprint seemed now inappropriate, a systematic revision a major task, a fresh approach a challenge to our younger theologians too exacting to meet the immediate need. This is a more modest endeavor—to look in my own way at some of the passages in the New Testament which speak to us of peace and war, violence and nonviolence, using Macgregor's enlightened discussions as a basis, and then to see these passages in the wider context of Christ's work as a whole. I of course am not a New Testament scholar in the sense in which Macgregor was a New Testament scholar: there is little danger of my being diverted by temporary and contemporary controversy. But I have tried to "keep in touch."

Having written these last words I must partially recant. It is impossible to write a Christian book in the 1970s without taking account of current Christian approaches. To ignore the new theology and the new morality would be to court irrelevance. I cannot omit situation ethics, God-as-the-depth-of-our-being, the death of God, religionless Christianity, and would not wish to do so, for I have learned from all these approaches. I cannot even omit Professor S.G.F. Brandon's peculiar incursion into historical fiction (based on the earlier work of R. Eisler), because it combines a very scholarly and compelling exposition of the political involvement of Jesus with a very unscholarly and uncompelling rejection of the central traditions of the New Testament at just this point. (I have no wish here to enter upon a systematic examination of Brandon's views. When the evidence for his thesis that

Jesus was a man of violence is extracted from behind the parade of learning it is very thin. It is typical of his methods that in *Jesus and the Zealots* a possibility on p. 57 has become without further evidence a probability on p. 269; for an example of really tendentious writing see pp. 340-1.) Fashions will change, and these references will date my book as much as references to the controversies of his own day have dated Macgregor's. If mine has half as long a life as his I shall be proud. Meantime I have tried to prevent the references from becoming too obtrusive, especially when they seem to me likely to be ephemeral.

One point should be made at the outset. There is no need to be apologetic about the close examination of individual passages of the New Testament in general and of the gospels in particular. For, in the first place, our proper understanding of the New Testament as a whole can only be built up out of the accurate interpretation of its component parts. In the second place, we have come within this century to see increasingly the nature and importance of those component parts. The gospels are in fact built up out of isolated passages: each of these is technically known as a pericope (four syllables: pe-ri-co-pe) or "cut-out." These were preserved in the Church for various reasons, and it is in some ways more meaningful to ask what was the context of a passage in the life of the church than what was its context in the life of Jesus. I do not want to overstate this. There are those who say that we cannot get behind the church to Jesus at all. This is to throw out the baby with the bathwater. Jesus stands behind the church: the church would not have been there had it not been for Jesus. The *pericopai* were handed down, not invented. The fundamental point is that it is reasonable and even scholarly to look at each on its merits.

In the third place, while we would not wish to argue to pacifism on the basis of isolated proof-texts, there are many who argue *against* pacifism on precisely this basis. These must be answered, courteously, accurately, persuasively. These pages suggest some of the answers.

And in the fourth place, there are certain strands in contemporary theology to which a close examination of passages in the New Testament is not amiss. Dietrich Bonhoeffer proffered a religionless Christianity, but his own life and thought were rooted in the Bible. Rudolf Bultmann demythologizes Christianity, but scrutinizes the New Testament to see what he has to demythologize. C.H. Dodd is an admirable example of a scholar whose contribution is based upon his profound and detailed understanding of the New Testament. Paul Altizer has proclaimed the death of God with the corollary that God emptied himself into Jesus; it follows that our commitment is to Jesus, and the New Testament is one of the places where we must seek him. The evangelicals have been seeking a more scholarly understanding of the scriptures they so deeply value. All these approaches suggest a reexamination of the New Testament.

I am no great believer in footnotes. I find that they distract a reader from the text, and are often a demonstration of learning rather than a genuine illustration. I have found of special value in understanding the New Testament George Caird's commentary on *Luke* in the Pelican series, and C.H. Dodd's now classic exposition of *Romans* in the Moffatt commentaries (conveniently reprinted by Fontana). William Barclay's commentaries are always lucid and helpful. Oscar Cullman's *The State in the New Testament* is a small book of profound insight and scholarship. I have drawn upon some things I have written elsewhere: the chapter on "The Early Church" and some parts of "The Way of Christ" from *The Enthronement of Love,* a closer consideration of "Agape" from *Moral Values in the Ancient World,* and the account of "Rondon and the Chavantes" from *Reconciliation Quarterly.* Except for the last the matter has been rethought and rewritten, though some of the phrases remain. I have also drawn on three contributions from my *Studies in Social Commitment,* all of which exercised considerable influence on my thinking, John Hick's "The Structure of the War Problem," E.L. Allen's "Commitment" and Geoffrey Nuttall's "The Church's Ministry of Suffering." The treatment of Reinhold Niebuhr is indebted to another of G.H.C. Macgregor's books, *The Relevance of an Impossible Ideal,* though I have made my own comments on Niebuhr elsewhere. Of recent books from a pacifist standpoint I have found James Douglass (an American Catholic) *The Non-Violent Cross* most helpful. But it would be impossible to acknowledge all I owe to those who have affected the thinking of these pages.

The title has been chosen after a lot of thought. I wanted it to be clear that this was a successor to Macgregor's *The New Testament Basis of Pacifism* without causing wanton confusion. In the 1970s nonviolence is a more favored term than pacifism, though of itself it is a negative term. I would like to have used Gandhi's *satyagraha,* soul-force, truth-force or love-force, but it imparts a different flavor. I also wanted to establish a link with my own *The Enthronement of Love.*

I owe thanks to many people: most particularly to Alison Andrews for her work with the typewriter, and to my wife Elnora for reading the manuscript, for compiling the indices, and for all her partnership in the adventures of Christian peacemaking. It is good that this book is now to

circulate more widely in America, and I am grateful to Richard Deats
and Olcutt Sanders for their help and encouragement. Those who wish
to know more about the adventures of Christian peacemaking should
write to the Fellowship of Reconciliation, Box 271, Nyack, New York
10960.

INTRODUCTION TO THE AMERICAN EDITION

In my twelve years of teaching Christian Social Ethics at Union
Theological Seminary in the Philippines, revolutionary movements were
having a strong impact throughout the islands as in many other parts of
the world. Christians were wrestling with the appeal of the "just
revolution," the modern counterpart of the "just war." This same
struggle continues, of course, not only in the developing nations but
wherever conscientious Christians attempt to relate their faith to the
pressing social issues of the day.

G.H.C. Macgregor wrote his classic *The New Testament Basis of
Pacifism* in 1936 at a time when the tragic memory of World War I was
still vivid and the impending horror of a second World War was
beginning to loom on the horizon. Macgregor helped many of his
generation see the utter incompatibility of the Christian faith and
warfare. Now, over four decades later, John Ferguson, another British
thinker, has provided us with a significant successor to Macgregor's
work, taking into account recent theological and biblical insights as well
as developments in the understanding and practice of nonviolence.

Ferguson is an able scholar who writes in a straightforward and
persuasive manner. He examines the New Testament foundation of
pacifism, the witness of the early church, and the political dimensions of
Jesus's ministry; he concludes with a moving statement on the way of
Christ for our own day and age.

The American Fellowship of Reconciliation is printing this edition
of *The Politics of Love* because we believe it is an important
contribution to the ongoing task of dealing faithfully and creatively with
violence and oppression and in building the beloved community.

Richard L. Deats
Executive Secretary
Fellowship of Reconciliation
Nyack, New York

July 10, 1979

THE NEW TESTAMENT
EVIDENCE

THE TEACHING OF JESUS IN THE GOSPELS

Matthew 5:38-48

"You have learned that they were told, 'An eye for an eye, and a tooth for a tooth.' But what I tell you is this: Do not set yourself against the man who wrongs you. If someone slaps you on the right cheek, turn and offer him your left. If a man wants to sue you for your shirt, let him have your coat as well. If a man in authority makes you go one mile, go with him two. Give when you are asked to give; and do not turn your back on a man who wants to borrow.

"You have learned that they were told, 'Love your neighbor, hate your enemy.' But what I tell you is this: Love your enemies and pray for your persecutors; only so can you be children of your heavenly Father, who makes his sun rise on good and bad alike, and sends the rain on the honest and the dishonest. If you love only those who love you, what reward can you expect? Surely the tax-gatherers do as much as that. And if you greet only your brothers, what is there extraordinary about that? Even the heathen do as much. You must therefore be all goodness, just as your heavenly Father is all good."

This passage comes from the teaching which Matthew presents as the Sermon on the Mount. It is a passage of considerable importance. We should note the following things about it.

(a) Matthew presents it as comprehensive teaching given to Jesus *to the disciples* (5:1-2). Whether or not this is an authentic tradition—the whole episode is "timeless" and the sequence of thought is not always clear if it were originally a connected discourse—it is clear that the church towards the end of the first century A.D. needed it as an expression, with the Lord's authority, of the way of life to be followed by committed Christians.

(b) The relationship of the New Testament or Covenant to the Old—of the way of life inaugurated by Jesus to the way associated with Sinai—is clear. "You have learned that they were told.... But I tell you this." The new way replaces the old. (Even today questioners sometimes say "After all, the Bible says An eye for an eye." This is not the way of Jesus.)

(c) It is still sometimes suggested that the way of life proclaimed in the

Sermon on the Mount is an *Interimsethik,* a temporary morality, related only to the brief period between the first coming of Christ and the final Day of the Lord, and therefore of no serious concern to the twentieth century. The more we think about this the less plausible it seems. For

(i) it is suggesting a degree of delusion in Jesus which would make it difficult to accept him as Lord and Master.

(ii) the more we see this as the ethic of the church fifty years after Jesus (a reasonable date for *Matthew*) the less it looks like an interim-ethic. At least the interim has outlasted many lifetimes!

(iii) we can indeed in these terms accept it as an ethic for the Christian disciple in the interim between the coming of Christ and the final Day of the Lord. If that Day is delayed for thousands of years, what matter for Him in whose sight a thousand years are but as yesterday (*Ps.* 90:4)?

(iv) more seriously and importantly, the way of life outlined in this passage is not at any point linked to the relativities of a temporary situation, but rooted in the very nature of God (5:45).

(d) The way of love will be discussed later. Here Jesus spells out the fact that it is comprehensive, and includes enemies. Some interpreters have accepted this as valid in personal relationships toward personal enemies, but not in political or group relations. The distinction would not have occurred to a Jew. The Greek word used (*echthros*) is the only word which could be used impartially for enemies in both a personal and a public sense. The reference to the man in authority who can impress your labor to carry his pack for one mile is an explicit reference to the Roman army of occupation.

(e) The NEB translation of 5:39 is misleading. There is no possible justification for translating "the man who wrongs *you,*" and it is difficult to see why the more familiar "resist," which is exactly right, has been changed to "set yourself against." The exact meaning is, however, not clear. The verb means "to make a stand against," as in battle. "Do not resist...." — whom, what or how? The Greek words could be neuter or masculine. If masculine, the injunction would read "Do not fight against the evil man," which makes sense in the context; it might mean, though I do not think it does, "Do not fight against the evil one," i.e. the devil, which does not really fit the context. If the phrase is neuter the obvious meaning is "Do not resist evil"; this is the familiar version, though it is hard to see just what it means. But it is just possible to translate "Do not make a stand by evil means." Now one effect of twentieth-century New Testament scholarship has been to make it less easy to say of passages in the gospels "This is Jesus" and of passages in the epistles "This is Paul," and to encourage us to say of both "This is the Christian Church." There *are* differences: Paul had a strong personality and an original mind. But both Paul and Matthew are drawing on traditions preserved in the Church, the same traditions. We can therefore look at the ethic of the Sermon on the Mount and the ethic of *Romans* side by side. We shall come to the latter in a moment. Here we may note that this phrase is there found in the neuter (*Rom.* 12:9; cf. 12:21) and the tenor of the teaching is that we are not to pay back evil for evil but to use good to defeat evil. We can be fairly certain that whatever the exact meaning, this is the purport of this passage.

(f) The last verse of the passage is also ambiguous. Here the NEB version is unexceptionable, but we may usefully draw out four different shades of meaning.

(i) There is first the meaning suggested by the familiar AV "perfect." God is the source of all good; our goodness must not be less than his perfection. God is love; our love must not be less than that seen in his nature.

This thought has scandalized, or been ignored by, those who are bitterly aware of our failures and sinfulness. Yet the words are there, and constitute a challenge. At the very least we dare not deliberately accept a lower standard. If we are children of God, the family likeness must appear.

It is worth noting that the verb is future: "You will be perfect." A future may be a form of command ("You will take this letter and you will deliver it in person") but it is a form we use only when we expect the command to be fulfilled. The NEB version conveys the meaning well.

(ii) The word may mean "all-embracing," "comprehensive." This fits the context well: we are to show love not only to our friends but to our enemies, not only to good men but to bad men, not only to those whom we expect to respond but to those whom we do not expect to respond.

(iii)) The word may mean "absolute," "unconditional." Here again the last point is vital. We may not say, "I will love a Roman or a Nazi on condition that he changes his spots." The love to which Christ calls us is unconditional.

(iv) The same word is used by Paul, in writing to Ephesus, of "mature manhood" (*Eph.* 4:13), "measured by nothing less than the full stature of Christ." This links with the first meaning, except that we are thinking not of God in his eternal nature, but of God revealed in

Christ. "Anyone who has seen me has seen the Father" (*Jn.* 14:9).

We may not choose one of these shades of meaning to the exclusion of the others.

(g) How literally are the injunctions to be taken? It would be foolish to suggest that if you are slapped on the *right* cheek you offer the other, but if you are slapped on the *left*, you can knock the man down, or like Battling Billson in P.G. Wodehouse's story, offer the other cheek, and then, when he hits that, punch him on the jaw ("A man has only two cheeks"). In fact, the *right* cheek is specified with a purpose. To strike you on the *right* cheek a man must use his left hand or the back of his hand, thereby adding insult to injury. It is a characteristically vivid illustration of a situation. To press the letter is to fall into the sort of legalism from which Jesus came to free us. To use this fact as an excuse for not taking the way of life seriously is apostasy.

Ned Richards was an American conscientious objector in the first world war. He felt that his life was too sheltered, that he must test his faith under fire as the soldiers tested theirs. He went to live in West Persia where there was continual strife, murder and sudden death. A company of armed marauding Kurds came to the mission house where Richards was with the women and children and one invalid man. They were surprised to be admitted instead of having to force their way in. They started looting. Richards saw, as he says in his record of his experiences, that to go the second mile, to add the cloak to the shirt, meant helping them to loot his own possessions. There is no doubt that his example of nonviolent love, his refusal to meet hostility with hostility, his active benevolence saved the lives of all in the house. But he did not undertake it for that reason. He undertook it because he took seriously and committed himself to the way of life exemplified in this passage.

Matthew 5:3-10

> When he saw the crowds he went up the hill. There he took his seat, and when his disciples had gathered round him he began to address them. And this is the teaching he gave:
>   "How blest are those who know that they are poor;
>   the kingdom of Heaven is theirs.
>   How blest are the sorrowful;
>   they shall find consolation.
>   How blest are those of a gentle spirit;
>   they shall have the earth for their possession.

How blest are those who hunger and thirst to see right prevail;
  they shall be satisfied.
How blest are those who show mercy;
  mercy shall be shown to them.
How blest are those whose hearts are pure;
  they shall see God.
How blest are the peacemakers;
  God shall call them his sons.
How blest are those who have suffered persecution for the
    cause of right;
  the kingdom of Heaven is theirs."

Matthew places the Beatitudes in the forefront of the conspectus of Christian teaching contained in the Sermon on the Mount. We should here notice the following things about these eight profound and pithy sayings.
(a) They all contrast apparent reality with true reality. They all declare the exaltation of those who would seem on the face of it to be the underdogs. This is part of the transvaluation effected by Jesus.
(b) In six of the sayings the exaltation is future, but in the first and last it is present; the kingdom is already theirs; they are in the kingdom.
(c) The opening word of each saying ("How blest" — in the Greek just "Blest") has sometimes been rendered "Happy" or "Fortunate." This is right in so far as it stresses a condition in this world, not "the other side of the stars." But NEB is right. The idea, in the *Psalms* (*Ps.* 1:1, etc.) and elsewhere, is the state of those who have a special commitment to God.
(d) Matthew's version of the Beatitudes is less material, more spiritual than Luke's (*Lk.* 6:20-23). In *Luke* the blessing is spoken over the needy and hungry; in *Matthew* over those who know their need of God (a paraphrase in NEB, not wholly easy to justify), and those who hunger to do what is right. It could be that both go back to Jesus. If only one is authentic, it is more likely to be Luke's.
  Christianity means social revolution:
    He has brought down monarchs from their thrones,
      but the humble have been lifted high.
    The hungry he has satisfied with good things,
      the rich sent empty away. (*Lk.* 1:52-53).
(e) There is an intimate connection between quality and reward: so much so that we might call it result rather than reward. Thus in some of the Beatitudes a hunger leads to fulfillment. Ask, and it shall be given

to you! A spirit of mercy breeds mercy; love kindles love, hatred hatred, violence violence, mercy mercy. To have purity of heart is to have clarity of vision over the things that matter: it is to see God. To know your need of God, to accept persecution for his sake is to take him as your king; it is to align yourself with the ultimate purposes of light. To be a peacemaker is to be like God, for in Hebrew the words "son of" are used to express likeness; it is to share in God's work.

(f) The qualities commended point in no way to armed resistance to evil. They call for gentleness of spirit, mercy, purity, suffering. Above all we are confronted with the words "How blest are the peacemakers." *Pacifist* means *peacemaker*. The true pacifist is not the man who says No to war but the man who says Yes to peace. The second may involve the first; too many have professed the first without practicing the second. These words indict pacifists by their failure to live up to their principles; do they not indict non-pacifists in principle and practice?

THE TEACHING OF JESUS IN THE EPISTLES AND ACTS

Romans 12:9-13, 14

Love in all sincerity, loathing evil and clinging to the good. Let love for our brotherhood breed warmth of mutual affection. Give pride of place to one another in esteem.

With unflagging energy, in ardor of spirit, serve the Lord.

Let hope keep you joyful; in trouble stand firm; persist in prayer.

Contribute to the needs of God's people, and practice hospitality.

Call down blessings on your persecutors—blessings, not curses.

With the joyful be joyful, and mourn with the mourners.

Have equal regard for one another. Do not be haughty, but go about with humble folk. Do not keep thinking how wise you are.

Never pay back evil for evil. Let your aims be such as all men count honorable. If possible, so far as it lies with you, live at peace with all men. My dear friends, do not seek revenge, but leave a place for divine retribution; for there is a text which reads, "Justice is mine, says the Lord, I will repay." But there is another text: "If your enemy is hungry, feed him; if he is thirsty, give him a drink;

by doing this you will heap live coals on his head." Do not let evil conquer you, but use good to defeat evil.

Every person must submit to the supreme authorities. There is no authority but by act of God, and the existing authorities are instituted by him; consequently anyone who rebels against authority is resisting a divine institution, and those who so resist have themselves to thank for the punishment they will receive. For government, a terror to crime, has no terrors for good behavior. You wish to have no fear of the authorities? Then continue to do right and you will have their approval, for they are God's agents working for your good. But if you are doing wrong, then you will have no cause to fear them; it is not for nothing that they hold the power of the sword, for they are God's agents of punishment, for retribution on the offender. That is why you are obliged to submit. It is an obligation imposed not merely by fear of retribution but by conscience. That is also why you pay taxes. The authorities are in God's service and to these duties they devote their energies.

Discharge your obligations to all men, pay tax and toll, reverence and respect, to those to whom they are due. Leave no claim outstanding against you, except that of mutual love. He who loves his neighbor has satisfied every claim of the law. For the commandments, "Thou shalt not commit adultery, thou shalt not kill, thou shalt not steal, nor shalt not covet," and any other commandment there may be, are all summed up in the one rule, "Love your neighbor as yourself." Love cannot wrong a neighbor; therefore the whole law is summed up in love.

In all this remember how critical the moment is. It is time for you to wake out of sleep, for deliverance is nearer to us now than it was when first we believed. It is far on in the night; day is near. Let us therefore throw off the deeds of darkness and put on our armor as soldiers of the light. Let us behave with decency as befits the day: no revelling or drunkenness, no debauchery or vice, no quarrels or jealousies! Let Christ Jesus himself be the armor that you wear; give no more thought to satisfying the bodily appetites.

This is a long passage, but it is essential to see it as a whole.
(a)   It is important to remember that *Romans* was written before any of our gospels achieved their present form. All the documents of the New Testament carry the mark of three influences.
   (i) There is the force of the individual writer.
   (ii) There is the local situation in which the document was written.

The letters reflect the condition of their recipients, and sometimes the atmosphere of the place where Paul was at the time. The gospels have often and reasonably been supposed to reflect the traditions of the place where they were written, *John* giving the traditions of Ephesus, for example.

(iii) There are the general traditions of the church.

This is important. *Romans* offers us the ethical traditions found within the church of a generation before *Matthew*. We are seeing them through the eyes of Paul in one, of Matthew in the other. The central tradition is the same, and *Romans* may properly be used as evidence of it.

(b) There is no stronger or clearer exposition of Christian pacifism than that in the twelfth chapter of *Romans*. The point does not need laboring. "Do not let evil conquer you, but use good to defeat evil." This is precisely what the Christian pacifist seeks to do, and the non-pacifist feels, however reluctantly, that he cannot do. The ethic of love is spelled out in its practical meaning.

(c) The concept of divine retribution, or, more literally, wrath, has been discussed in the opening passages of the letter. It is a vivid expression of the fact that the universe is a moral universe. If we behave wrongly, the world goes wrong, for ourselves and others. This is an ultimate fact of life.

(d) The opening words of the thirteenth chapter have, however, caused difficulty to some. It states that the existing authorities are instituted by God and everyone should submit to them. Does it not follow then that their use of capital punishment and war is equally instituted by God, and that the Christian should submit to military conscription?

(i) A simple point, first, but an important one. Paul suggests that government is a God-given institution, not that the decisions of those in power are always approved by God. Non-pacifists who make much of this passage do not really believe that they should do anything those in power decree. On the contrary they extol Dietrich Bonhoeffer for his act of violent rebellion against Hitler. Socrates, ordered by the Thirty Dictators to arrest the innocent but wealthy Leon, was surely right to turn on his heel and walk away.

(ii) The chapter divisions in the New Testament do not belong to the original writings; they are a later addition, and not always divinely inspired. But the opening of the thirteenth chapter must be read in the context of the unequivocal pacifism which ends the twelfth.

(iii) The words must be set in political context. They are addressed to Christians in Rome, many of whom at this time must have been Jewish in nationality. The Jews were continually on the verge of armed rebellion against the Romans. There were disturbances in the capital in Claudius's reign, "on the instigation of Chrestus," says the Roman historian Suetonius: it looks as if his version was garbled and Christians were involved. Seen in context, Paul's words become clear. They are a warning against violent resistance, and a plea for the revolutionary methods of nonviolent love.

(iv) C.H. Dodd summed up the matter well: "The Christian takes no part in the administration of a retributive system; but, in so far as it serves moral ends, he must submit to it. He himself lives by a higher principle, and he obeys the Government, not because he fears the retribution which follows on disobedience, but because his conscience bids him do so." The practice of the early church, as presented by the apologists, was to be loyal citizens in all the normal obligations of citizenship, to outdo their fellow-citizens in the quality of their service, but to stand aside with a clear No if the State made demands which cut across their prior loyalty to God.

1 *John* 4:7-21

Dear friends, let us love one another, because love is from God. Everyone who loves is a child of God and knows God, but the unloving know nothing of God. For God is love; and his love was disclosed to us in this, that he sent his only Son into the world to bring us life. The love I speak of is not our love for God, but the love he showed to us in sending his Son as the remedy for the defilement of our sins. If God thus loved us, dear friends, we in turn are bound to love one another. Though God has never been seen·by any man, God himself dwells in us if we love one another; his love is brought to perfection within us.

Here is the proof that we dwell in him and he dwells in us: he has imparted his Spirit to us. Moreover, we have seen for ourselves, and we attest that the Father sent the Son to be the savior of the world, and if a man acknowledges that Jesus is the Son of God, God dwells in him and he dwells in God. Thus we have come to know and believe the love which God has for us.

God is love; he who dwells in love is dwelling in God, and God in him. This is for us the perfection of love, to have confidence on the day of judgment, and this we can have because even in this

world we are as he is. There is no room for fear in love; perfect
love banishes fear. For fear brings with it the pains of judgment,
and anyone who is afraid has not attained to love in its perfection.
We love because he loved us first. But if a man says, "I love God,"
while hating his brother, he is a liar. If he does not love the brother
whom he has seen, it cannot be that he loves God whom he has not
seen. And indeed this command comes to us from Christ himself:
that he who loves God must also love his brother.

This is one of the greatest of all accounts of Christian love. John
makes four major assertions.
(a) Love is the very nature of God. Love is the power which pulsates
through the universe. Love is the depth of our being. Love is the only
way the world will work. Love is the only way in which we can find our
true selves. All this is implicit in the words "God is love."
(b) God's love is incomplete until we show love. This is an astonishing
thing for John to say, but he says it: God's love is "brought to perfection
in us."
(c) It is useless our claiming to love God unless we love our brothers.
(d) If we are afraid of anyone or anything there is something lacking in
our love.

Romans 5:7-8

Even for a just man one of us would hardly die, though perhaps
for a good man one might actually brave death; but Christ died for
us while we were yet sinners, and that is God's proof of his love
towards us.

This well-known passage is important for the understanding of
love. For
(a) love is shown towards all men, bad men, sinners. It does not
depend upon response from the other.
(b) love is shown in suffering, not in the infliction of suffering.

1 *Corinthians* 13:4-7

Love is patient; love is kind and envies no one. Love is never
boastful, nor conceited, nor rude; never selfish, not quick to take
offense. Love keeps no score of wrongs; does not gloat over other
men's sins, but delights in the truth. There is nothing love cannot

face; there is no limit to its faith, its hope, and its endurance.

This is the most famous of all passages about Christian love. "There is nothing love cannot face; there is no limit to its faith, its hope, and its endurance." If we take this seriously can we lay aside love and go to war? No one today seriously suggests that we can go to war in love.

Galatians 5:19-25

> Anyone can see the kind of behavior that belongs to the lower nature: fornication, impurity, and indecency; idolatry and sorcery; quarrels, a contentious temper, envy, fits of rage, selfish ambitions, dissensions, party intrigues, and jealousies; drinking bouts, orgies, and the like. I warn you, as I warned you before, that those who behave in such ways will never inherit the kingdom of God.
> But the harvest of the Spirit is love, joy, peace, patience, kindness, goodness, fidelity, gentleness, and self-control. There is no law dealing with such things as these. And those who belong to Christ Jesus have crucified the lower nature with its passions and desires. If the Spirit is the source of our life, let the Spirit also direct our course.

In this passage Paul contrasts the way of man's lower nature with the way of the Spirit of Christ. It is hardly necessary to comment. But we may notice that the sin called dissension means literally "standing apart." Separation is sin. And we cannot evade the fact that peace is one of the chief fruits of the Spirit.

How will the Spirit, whose harvest is thus identified, seek to change the world? How will the Spirit, whose harvest is thus identified, seek to meet an aggressor or a dictator?

James 4:12

> There is only one lawgiver and judge, the One who is able to save life and destroy it. So who are you to judge your neighbor?

James is speaking of slanderous gossip, but his words have a wider application.

(a) When James speaks of law he has in mind what he calls the sovereign law (2:8) "Love your neighbor as yourself."

(b) We are not to judge our fellows. James is of course thinking of the Sermon on the Mount: "Pass no judgment and you will not be judged" (*Mt.* 7:1). One of the problems of war is that we are prosecutors, judges and executioners; the problem is acute for those who stand on some doctrine of "the just war," for they are in conscience bound to pass judgment before fighting, and they are in conscience bound not to do so.

(c) With God is the power to exact death and with him alone.

James 3:17-18

> But the wisdom from above is in the first place pure; and then peace-loving, considerate, and open to reason; it is straightforward and sincere, rich in mercy and in the kindly deeds that are its fruit. True justice is the harvest reaped by peacemakers from seeds sown in a spirit of peace.

(a) Of all the books of the New Testament *James* shows the greatest concern about how we live. It is an intensely practical book; Luther did not like it because it stressed acts more than faith. But it seems very close to the teaching of Jesus in the gospels, not least in the Sermon on the Mount.

(b) This passage has to do with wisdom. It is the universal testimony of the Bible, Old and New Testaments, that wisdom comes from God. *Ecclesiasticus* begins with the words:

> All wisdom is from the Lord;
> wisdom is with him forever.

We are too apt to exalt our own worldly wisdom. Paul has strong words for those who call the way of God impractical folly (1*Cor.* 1:18-24); God's folly is wiser than man's wisdom.

(c) This passage is notable for its positive emphasis on peace, peace meaning a right relationship between men and God, and between men and men, individuals and groups.

(d) James is here spelling out in concrete this-worldly terms the blessing on the peacemakers in the Beatitudes (*Mt.* 5:9).

(e) Some twentieth-century Christian thinkers, such as William Temple, have suggested that justice must come before love and before peace, that we must first achieve justice, and then we can go on to love and peace. James says exactly the opposite. Only the peacemakers can harvest true justice.

1 *Peter* 3:16-18

> Keep your conscience clear, so that when you are abused, those who malign your Christian conduct may be put to shame. It is better to suffer for well-doing, if such should be the will of God, than for doing wrong. For Christ also died for our sins once and for all. He, the just, suffered for the unjust, to bring us to God.

This is an important passage for our understanding of the Christian life.

(a) "Keep your conscience clear." The pacifist is sometimes accused of guarding his own conscience at the expense of others: Ernest Bevin said something similar of George Lansbury in singularly brutal terms. This is a total misapprehension. The pacifist is not concerned with saving his own soul; he is concerned with God's way of saving the world. Peter says that to do right unwaveringly sooner or later convicts and convinces those who mock. The Christian life is the best argument for Christianity. Albert Luthuli and Martin Niemoeller and Danilo Dolci and Martin Luther King and Helder Camara are the great arguments that the pacifist understanding of Christ is the true one.

(b) It is better to suffer for doing right than for doing wrong. Christ suffered in this way, and Peter gives him the Messianic title of "the just," and in so doing put his way of suffering in a political context. In choosing to suffer wrong rather than commit wrong we follow in the footsteps of Christ.

1 *Peter* 3:8-9

> To sum up: be one in thought and feeling, all of you; be full of brotherly affection, kindly and humble-minded. Do not repay wrong with wrong, or abuse with abuse; on the contrary, retaliate with blessing, for a blessing is the inheritance to which you yourselves have been called.

Here is Peter's summary of the marks of the Christian life: unity, sympathy, brotherly love, compassion, humility, and the refusal to meet evil with evil. It is true that Peter's first thought is within the church, true too that he is thinking primarily of individual and personal relations. But will the person who has put on Christ behave differently to non-Christians? Can he assent to the vast impersonality of destruction which is war?

Acts 4:19

  "Is it right in God's eyes for us to obey you rather than God?"

Acts 5:29

  "We must obey God rather than men."

  This was how the church spread.
(a) The disciples did not ask "Is it safe?" They asked "Is it God's will?" (H.G. Wells once rather surprisingly said, "The trouble with so many people is that the voice of their neighbors sounds louder than the voice of God.") They did not ask, "What does human wisdom suggest?" They asked, "What does divine folly enjoin?"
(b) In all they have Jesus in mind, and in the second passage this is explicit. They go on to tell how Jesus was exalted after being executed. He is leader and savior. Out of suffering love comes a new way of life and health for men. They are certain that suffering in obedience to God's will becomes the channel of God's power to transform the world.

2 *Corinthians* 4:8-10

  Hard-pressed on every side, we are never hemmed in; bewildered, we are never at our wit's end; hunted, we are never abandoned to our fate; struck down, we are not left to die. Wherever we go we carry death with us in our body, the death that Jesus died, that in this body also life may reveal itself, the life that Jesus lives.

  This marvelous passage speaks for itself.
(a) The Christian must expect persecution. This is the promise of the gospels, and it is a sign of our ineffectiveness that most of us have not experienced it. Not that we should provoke martyrdom; the church has rightly discouraged that, which usually springs from a diseased psychology. But if we were consistently doing right, consistently seeking God's will, consistently following Jesus, we would offend entrenched privilege more than we do. But we would also see God's power at work

through our obedience and through the love he has kindled in us. We could not be crushed, because we should be in the kingdom.

(b) The way for the Christian, the way which Paul took, is exemplified by the death of Jesus; it is the way of the cross. And that, we must repeat, is the way which refuses to meet evil with evil and violence with violence, but which encounters them with a steadfast love and the willingness, if it be God's will, to suffer.

(c) This suffering is redemptive. Again, we must repeat, the pacifist does not seek to save his own miserable soul. The way he chooses is life for others through his own death, if that be God's will.

2 *Corinthians* 13:11-14

> And now, my friends, farewell. Mend your ways; take our appeal to heart; agree with one another; live in peace; and the God of love and peace will be with you. Greet one another with the kiss of peace. All God's people send you greetings.
>
> The grace of the Lord Jesus Christ, and the love of God, and the fellowship of the Holy Spirit, be with you all.

It would be foolish to build any extravagant theories on the final greeting of a letter — as if a historian of A.D. 4000 were to analyse our "Yours faithfully." Still, Paul's greetings were not casual, and it is worth noting the association of love and peace here, as in *Galatians* 5:22. It would be wholly extravagant to suggest that we might put "God is peace" alongside "God is love" (1 *Jn*. 4:9). Paul does in fact elsewhere say of Jesus "he is himself our peace" (*Eph*. 2:14).

Plainly Paul is thinking primarily of the divisions within the church at Corinth; he is not thinking of international relations. The word *shalom* in Hebrew is richer than the Greek *eirene* or the English *peace*. Equally we shall not do wrong to say that just as love starts from the nature and being of God and finds its human expression in our response to God, in the fellowship of the church (*Jn*. 13:34), in relations with the neighbor (*Lk*. 10:27-28), and in meeting the enemy (*Mt*. 5:44), so peace starts from the nature and being of God and finds its human expressions in ever-widening circles till it embraces all mankind.

The final "grace" is so familiar that we do not think about it. It starts from Jesus and the free gift of his loving-kindness shown in his suffering (*Rom*. 3:24-25; *Tit*. 2:11-14). This is, definitely and clearly, the grace that comes to us from Jesus Christ. The other phrases are ambiguous. The love of God can mean the love which God shows for us or the love which we offer to God. Both are New Testament thoughts (1 *Jn.* 4:9-11; *Lk.* 10:27). No doubt Paul is praying for God to show his love for the Corinthians; but he is also praying that they will respond with their love, which can be sincerely shown only in the love of their visible brethren (1 *Jn.* 4:20-21). So with the last phrase, the fellowship of (not "in" NEB) the Holy Spirit. This can indeed mean that the church shares the Spirit, that all its members have a share of the Spirit. But it can also mean the fellowship produced by the Spirit; it can mean that where the Spirit is at work, the barriers between human beings are broken down. Those who receive the grace of Jesus live continually in the power and presence of the Spirit of Jesus, and this transforms all their relations.

THE MINISTRY OF JESUS

Matthew 4:1-11

Jesus was then led away by the Spirit into the wilderness, to be tempted by the devil.

For forty days and nights he fasted, and at the end of them he was famished. The tempter approached him and said, "If you are the Son of God, tell these stones to become bread." Jesus answered, "Scripture says, 'Man cannot live on bread alone; he lives on every word that God utters.' "

The devil then took him to the Holy City and set him on the parapet of the temple. "If you are the Son of God," he said, "throw yourself down; for Scripture says, 'He will put his angels in charge of you, and they will support you in their arms, for fear you should strike your foot against a stone.' " Jesus answered him, "Scripture says again, 'You are not to put the Lord your God to the test.' "

Once again, the devil took him to a very high mountain, and showed him all the kingdoms of the world in their glory. "All these," he said, "I will give you, if you will only fall down and do me homage." But Jesus said, "Begone, Satan; Scripture says, 'You shall do homage to the Lord your God and worship him alone.' "

Then the devil left him, and the angels appeared and waited on him.

The temptations are an important key to the ministry of Jesus. Three temptations are recorded.

(a) Jesus is tempted to use his powers for selfish ends, to satisfy his own hunger. His answer is the answer he was later to give his followers, "No, do not ask anxiously, 'What are we to eat? What are we to drink? What shall we wear?'... Set your mind on God's kingdom and his justice before everything else, and all the rest will come to you as well" (6:31-33).

(b) Jesus is tempted to use his powers to work a demonstrative miracle. His answer is that God's power is not to be challenged and tested but trusted.

(c) It is the third temptation which concerns us here. It is the temptation to achieve political power by the devil's means and on the devil's conditions. Briefly:

(i) We must remember that one of the devil's titles was "Prince of the World."

(ii) Jesus's reply is a clear answer to those who say that the way of God cannot be applied to politics. We are not to be governed by worldly wisdom; we are to serve God, and him alone.

(iii) Jesus's answer must further be seen in the light of the confidence in God's power already expressed. A favorite question to pacifists begins, "What would happen if. . . ." Jesus's answer rings down the ages, "You shall not tempt the Lord your God."

(iv) Jesus's answer is to be seen in its political context. G.B. Caird writes on the corresponding passage in *Luke* (4:5-8): "Among the Jews there was a party known as the Zealots who expected the Messiah to be a conqueror who would lead them in a war of liberation, and there were scriptures which endorsed their view (*Ps.* 2:9; *Zech.* 12:7-9). Were they perhaps the practical men, the realists who would get results while the visionary was still dreaming his dreams? It is good to be realistic, but the greatest reality is God, and true realism is to believe that only God's purpose is worth striving for and only God's methods can achieve it. . . . To worship God is to trust him and leave the results in his hands."

Mark 8:27-38

Jesus and his disciples set out for the villages of Caesarea Philippi. On the way he asked his disciples, "Who do men say I am?" They answered, "Some say John the Baptist, others Elijah, others one of the prophets." "And you," he asked, "who do you say I am?" Peter replied: "You are the Messiah." Then he gave them strict orders not to tell anyone about him; and he began to teach them that the Son of Man had to undergo great sufferings, and to be rejected by the elders, chief priests, and doctors of the law; to be put to death, and to rise again three days afterwards. He spoke about it plainly. At this Peter took him by the arm and began to rebuke him. But Jesus turned round, and, looking at his disciples, rebuked Peter. "Away with you, Satan," he said; "you think as men think, not as God thinks."

Then he called the people to him as well as his disciples, and said to them, "Anyone who wishes to be a follower of mine must leave self behind; he must take up his cross, and come with me. Whoever cares for his own safety is lost; but if a man will let himself be lost for my sake and for the Gospel, that man is safe. What does a man gain by winning the whole world at the cost of his true self? What can he give to buy that self back? If anyone is ashamed of me and mine in this wicked and godless age, the Son of Man will be ashamed of him, when he comes in the glory of his Father and of the holy angels.

This is a passage of vital significance.

(a) Peter acclaims Jesus as Messiah, and Jesus does not refuse the designation. In the fuller version in *Matthew* he praises Peter for it and explicitly accepts it (*Mt.* 16:13-20). The Messiah was to be the national leader and was expected by the majority to lead a successful violent resistance movement.

(b) Jesus immediately reveals himself a Messiah of a very different color. So far as we can see he was the first person to identify the Messiah with the Suffering Servant of Deutero-Isaiah, who conquers through suffering (*Is.* 52:13-53, 12). The Son of Man *had* to suffer; there was no other way. The Greek word is found in apocalyptic literature; it shows God's will and God's way. The way of man is violence, the way of God is service and suffering.

(c) Peter cannot understand this and protests. Jesus's answer is "Away with you, Satan." The language is that which Jesus used in rejecting the third temptation, as the NEB, which is unfortunately not strong on consistency, does not make clear. In trying to turn Jesus from the way of suffering to the more familiar concept of the Messiah, Peter is renewing the temptation to achieve political power by the devil's means and on the devil's terms, and indeed Luke in his version of the temptation says that "the devil departed, *biding his time*" (*Lk.* 4:13). The time came at Caesarea Philippi.

(d) Immediately after, Jesus says publicly: "Anyone who wishes to be a follower of mine must leave self behind, he must take up his cross, and come with me." It is hard to see what this means except in terms of a choice. T.W. Manson has suggested that when Jesus speaks of the Son of Man he is not just referring to himself but is using, in accordance with common prophetic practice, a single figure to connote a community, the new Israel, the faithful Remnant, the creative minority, Jesus with his disciples. The same is true of the figure of the Suffering Servant, who in some sense personifies the people of God and alternates between individual and community (*Is.* 44:21; 49:3). Jesus, as we have seen, has the Servant in mind. Here he invites not just his immediate disciples but any who will follow. But the way to which he invites them is the way of the cross not the way of the sword, the way of suffering rather than the way of inflicting suffering on others. This is in fact the choice. The

church preserved these words, having understood their meaning as
Peter and the others at Caesarea Philippi could not fully understand,
because by the time the gospels were written the words were fulfilled in
Jesus. They preserved these words as a standing injunction to all who
wish to be followers of Jesus, to eschew the way of violence and accept
instead the way of suffering, nonviolent love which took Jesus to the
cross.

Luke 9:52-56

> They set out and went into a Samaritan village to make arrange-
> ments for him; but the villagers would not have him because he
> was making for Jerusalem. When the disciples James and John saw
> this they said, "Lord, may we call down fire from heaven to burn
> them up, as Elijah did?" But he turned and rebuked them. "You do
> not know," he said, "to what spirit you belong; for the Son of Man
> did not come to destroy men's lives but to save them."

This episode took place when Jesus had turned to Jerusalem to be
"taken up" as Elijah was. Jesus's actual reply is not found in the best
manuscripts, but all our manuscripts record the fact of the rebuke.
G.B. Caird's comment is (as always) superbly good: "James and John
wanted to emulate Elijah (2 *Kings* 1:9-16); but we must recognize that
in this respect Elijah was typical of the whole Old Testament, which
knew no other way of dealing with enemies of Israel than to call down
God's curse upon them. This is why Elijah had to disappear from the
mountain to give place to Jesus, with his new way of loving his enemies
and dying for them, and to the new conception of God which that way
implied. It is, however, an impressive testimony to the power of Jesus
that the two brothers did not doubt their own ability in his name to call
down fire from heaven."

Bear this in mind and then think of Hiroshima and Nagasaki;
think of the fire-bombing of Dresden with "conventional" weapons.

> And the ray from that heat came soundless, shook the sky
> As if in search of food, and squeezed the stems
> Of all that grows on the earth till they were dry
> — And drank the marrow of the bone:
> The eyes that saw, the lips that kissed, are gone
> Or black as thunder lie and grin at the murdered Sun.

So Edith Sitwell in her "Three Poems of the Atomic Age." A voice still
cries "You do not know to what spirit you belong."

Abraham Lincoln once said, "Do I not destroy my enemies when I make them my friends?" But even if the hand of friendship fails, we who are called to Christ's work are called not to destroy lives but to save them.

Matthew 21:1-9

> They were now nearing Jerusalem; and when they reached Bethany at the Mount of Olives, Jesus sent two disciples with these instructions: "Go to the village opposite, where you will at once find a donkey tethered with her foal beside her; untie them, and bring them to me. If anyone speaks to you, say, 'Our Master needs them'; and he will let you take them at once." This was in fulfillment of the prophecy which said, "Tell the daughter of Zion, 'Here is your king, who comes to you in gentleness, riding on an ass, riding on the foal of a beast of burden.' "
>
> The disciples went and did as Jesus had directed, and brought the donkey and her foal; and they laid their cloaks on them and Jesus mounted. Crowds of people carpeted the road with their cloaks, and some cut branches from the trees to spread in his path. Then the crowds that went ahead and the others that came behind raised the shout: "Hosanna to the Son of David! Hosanna in the heavens!"

The nature of Jesus's entry into Jerusalem is of some importance to our understanding of his mission. We have seen that he accepted identification with the Messiah, but immediately went on to teach about a new way, the way of suffering. His triumphal entry into Jerusalem is the entry of a king; the clothes spread along the road are homage to a king; the title "Son of David" is a royal title; the palm branches (*Jn.* 12:13) recalled the rising of the Maccabees. Indeed the attitude of the crowd recalls a passage in *The Psalms of Solomon* (17:23-27):

> Behold, O Lord, and raise up their King, the son of David,
>> at the time thou hast appointed, O God,
>> to reign over Israel thy servant.
> Gird him with strength to shatter wicked rulers.
>> Cleanse Jerusalem from the Gentiles who trample it and destroy.
> In wisdom, in justice, may he thrust out sinners from God's heritage,
>> crush the arrogance of the sinner like a potter's crocks,

> crush his whole substance with an iron mace,
> blot out the lawless Gentiles with a word,
> put the Gentiles to flight with his threats!

The relevant Gentiles were the Romans. But Jesus rejected that part of the scriptural tradition which depicted the Messiah as buckling on his sword and riding to war on a white charger. He chose that part of prophecy which he would fulfill. If was a passage from *Zechariah* (9:9-10), which depicts the Messiah coming to Jerusalem humble, mounted on an ass (NEB unfortunately did not coordinate its Old Testament with its New Testament). And the next verse runs:

> He shall banish chariots from Ephraim
> and war-horses from Jerusalem;
> the warrior's bow shall be banished.
> He shall speak peaceably to every nation,
> and his rule shall extend from sea to sea,
> from the River to the ends of the earth.

A new Messiah, standing not for war and military victory but for disarmament and peace.

Matthew 26:51-52

> At that moment one of those with Jesus reached for his sword and drew it, and he struck at the High Priest's servant and cut off his ear. But Jesus said to him, "Put up your sword. All who take the sword die by the sword."

Revelation 13:10

> Whoever takes the sword to kill, by the sword he is bound to be killed.

We can reasonably put these passages side by side. *Revelation* is usually dated to about A.D. 95, and we can see the passage there is echoing the passage from the gospels.

(a) The passage from the gospels depicts the moment when Jesus fulfills the choice which he laid before his followers at Caesarea Philippi. At this moment he could have raised the standard of violent revolt. He did not do so. He went to the cross.

There is an interesting speculation here about Judas's motives. The meaning of the name Iscariot is uncertain, but some scholars have supposed it to be a corruption of the Latin *sicarius* or "dagger-man," a member of the violent resistance. Certainly Jesus must have attracted some members of this group, including no doubt Simon the Zealot, who would hope that they had found the nationalist leader whom they were seeking. Now the betrayal of Jesus by Judas has always been a puzzle, for the sum of thirty silver pieces is nugatory. Some have supposed that Judas was expecting after the triumphal entry into Jerusalem and the Cleansing of the Temple that the revolt would begin. When Jesus showed no signs of taking a violent initiative, Judas tried to force his hand. But Jesus accepted arrest and death rather than embark on a violence which was not God's will or way. Of course this is mere speculation about Jesus, but it is speculation which makes sense.

(b) Some advocates of non-pacifism have tried to see in these words a justification for war. They have argued that if aggressors, say the Nazis, are to perish by the sword it is the moral duty of defenders to have swords by which they perish. Nothing could be further from the proper interpretation of this passage. Jesus is making a simple statement of fact. Violence tends to provoke counter-violence, just as love tends to kindle love. And the violence provoked often exceeds the original violence; violence in other words tends to escalate. This is not a justification of those who are provoked; only a simple statement of historical fact.

(c) But it is precisely the defensive use of violence which is here condemned. The words are not spoken to an aggressor, a Hitler or a gangster. They are spoken to a loyal follower who misguidedly seeks to use violence to defend an innocent man from wrongful violence. They are in fact the clearest possible condemnation of all wars, however "defensive" or "just."

(d) This is how the early church understood the words. Tertullian in his treatise *On Patience* declared that at this moment in Gethsemane Jesus "cursed the works of the sword forever after." In another treatise *On Idolatry* he spells out the meaning of this more fully: "How shall the Christian wage war, how indeed shall he even be a soldier in peace-time, without the sword which the Lord has taken away? For although soldiers had come to John and received the form of their rule, although even a centurion had believed, the Lord afterwards in disarming Peter unbuckled every soldier."

Romans 8:18-25

For I reckon that the sufferings we now endure bear no comparison with the splendor, as yet unrevealed, which is in store for us. For the created universe waits with eager expectation for God's sons to be revealed. It was made the victim of frustration, not by its own choice, but because of him who made it so; yet always there was hope, because the universe itself is to be freed from the shackles of mortality and enter upon the liberty and splendor of the children of God. Up to the present, we know, the whole created universe groans in all its parts as if in the pangs of childbirth. Not only so, but even we, to whom the Spirit is given as firstfruits of the harvest to come, are groaning inwardly while we wait for God to make us his sons and set our whole body free. For we have been saved, though only in hope. Now to see is no longer to hope: why should a man endure and wait for what he already sees? But if we hope for something we do not yet seen, then, in waiting for it, we show our endurance.

This wonderful passage is included here for one reason. It is one of the greatest expressions of the constructive value of suffering. Jesus showed that the way of God was to reach out to mankind, to sinners, to men of violence, with an unquenchable love, and if neither words nor actions should win them, to suffer. And that suffering, freely undertaken in obedience to the will of God, was redemptive, constructive, transforming. In suffering he shows his kingship; he reigns from the cross.

In this passage Paul shows how deeply he has understood this fact. Suffering is the calling of the Christian disciple. He knows this: he knows that loyalty and commitment are shown in endurance. Jesus had said as much (*Mk*. 13:13). And he knows that the suffering is the channel through which new life enters the world. So he uses the metaphor of childbirth. The mother suffers pain, but through that pain a new life is born. Jesus suffered crucifixion, but it freed him from the straitjacket of a single human body (*Lk*. 12:50 "I have a baptism to undergo, and what constraint I am under until the ordeal is over!"), and through that crucifixion the Holy Spirit entered the world (*Jn*. 16:7 "If I do not go, your Advocate will not come"). The Christian disciple suffers, and out of that suffering is born the liberty and splendor of the sons of God.

We have a choice. The way of Jesus is the way of love, nonviolence and redemptive suffering. The way of the world rejects this as folly and weakness. But "the foolishness of God is wiser than men, and the weakness of God is stronger than men" (1 *Cor*. 1:25 AV against NEB which is simply wrong). One is tempted to say with Joshua of old:

"choose here and now whom you will worship" (*Josh.* 24:15).

Hebrews 2:10

> It was clearly fitting that God for whom and through whom all things exist should, in bringing many sons to glory, make the leader who delivers them perfect through sufferings.

This is a passage of great wealth of meaning, and if I treat it only briefly, that is no indication of its importance. It is not an isolated passage: it is a summary expression of a very important part of the thought of this letter.

(a) The suffering of Jesus was a stumbling-block to the Jews' acceptance of him as Messiah (1 *Cor.* 1:23); they had not come to equate the Messiah with the Suffering Servant. This letter was written to Jewish Christians, and the point made it substantial.

(b) The writer asserts that it was fitting for God to use suffering as a means to fulfillment, the word "God" is not in the Greek, which has simply "he," but the meaning is right. It is, however, worth noting that this is the exact language used by John of the Word, "through him all things came to be" (*Jn.* 1:3). It is the very nature of the creative power of God: it is a part of his plan for the world. The suffering of Jesus is not brought about by some accident of history, or the limitations of this material world; it is appropriate to the very nature of God.

(c) The word "leader," *archegos*, is as ambiguous in Greek as in English. It may mean "founder" or "originator," but it also has a military ring, and the AV "Captain" is not wrong. This is an allusion to the Messianic hope of a military liberator, but in the nature of God the deliverance is through suffering.

(d) The idea of the completeness or perfection occurs elsewhere in the New Testament. It is the limitless goodness demanded in the Sermon on the Mount (*Mt.* 5:48). It is the mature manhood for which Paul calls (*Eph.* 4:13). In other words this "perfection" is not something apposite to Christ but irrelevant to us. Christ is an example to us of our calling. If we would share in the work of bringing many sons to glory we must expect our way to lie through sufferings.

SOME PASSAGES WHICH HAVE CAUSED
DIFFICULTY

John 2:13-16

As it was near the time of the Jewish Passover, Jesus went up to Jerusalem. There he found in the temple the dealers in cattle, sheep, and pigeons, and the money-changers seated at their tables. Jesus made a whip of cords and drove them out of the temple, sheep, cattle, and all. He upset the tables of the money-changers, scattering their coins.

Much has been built on this passage by some interpreters. It is important to read it dispassionately.

(a) We must mention, to dismiss, Professor S.G.F. Brandon's fantastic view that the brief story in the gospels conceals a major military takeover of the temple as part of a movement of violent revolt. There is no trace of this outside Professor Brandon's imagination. The Roman garrison overlooked the temple courtyard to suppress riots. The physical disturbance must have been very minor. We must understand what is before us.

(b) There is no reason to underplay Jesus's anger. Harry Emerson Fosdick in his once famous book *The Manhood of the Master* had a whole study entitled "The Master's Indignation." Anger is one of the sinews of the soul; it spurs us to remedy wrongs, to change the world. There is a New Testament word, often rendered "gentleness" (e.g. 2 *Cor.* 10:1; *Gal.* 5:22); but Aristotle defines it as the mean between uncontrolled anger and the total absence of anger. Indifference is not a Christian virtue.

What marks Jesus's anger off from ours is that he is never angry for himself, always for others. Even knowing that there is a subtle temptation to rationalize an anger which is really selfish by pretending that it is exercised in defense of others. We are inconvenienced by a strike; we fulminate against the hardship to old people, but if we were not at the receiving end we would not think twice about others. "There are times when I do well to be angry," said George Matheson, "but I have mistaken the times."

(c) Our picture of the Cleansing of the Temple is colored by paintings by El Greco and others, which portray Jesus flailing a formidable whip and driving the men cowering before him. There is nothing of this in the gospel-narrative.

(i) The story is told in all four gospels; only John mentions a whip at all.

(ii) The AV "small cords" is better than the NEB "cords," though it is possible that both are wrong and that he took the belts from his disciples' coats and improvised an instrument with them. But however the instrument was devised it was not a weapon of offense.

(iii) The meaning of the Greek is really quite clear. The AV "he drove them all out of the temple, and the sheep, and the oxen" is wrong. The NEB is right, but slightly ambiguous. A clumsy but literal rendering would be "he drove them all, i.e. the sheep and cattle, out of the temple." There is no evidence at all that the improvised whip was used against men. It was a herdsman's instrument to shepherd the animals away.

(iv) In the corresponding passage in *Mark* the word used of dispensing the traders is wrongly translated "driving out" in NEB (11:15), and would be better rendered "told them to go" or "sent them away."

(d) We can thus identify the nature of Jesus's action.

(i) He shows blazing anger.

(ii) He uses scorching words.

(iii) He acts to change the situation.

(iv) He behaves violently towards *things*, tables and coins.

(v) There is no evidence of violent behavior against people.

(vi) Even if we go beyond the evidence and argue that there must have been some kind of forcible treatment of the people there is not destructive violence. There is nothing here which could form the remotest justification of war.

(e) There is one additional point. When Mark tells the story (11:15-19) he shows us Jesus quoting the scripture "My house shall be called a house of prayer *for all the nations*" and adding "But you have made it a robbers' cave." The scene is the Court of the Gentiles. A non-Jew might not penetrate further. Here was the end of his pilgrimage. Here he would want to worship, to meditate. And here was the chatter of the marketplace and the cynicism of those to whom religion was a means of money-making. Jesus's act was an act for the non-Jew. It was an act of internationalism. But, further, the word for "robbers" was a common nickname of the violently nationalistic Zealots. The Zealots, as C.H. Dodd has put it, expected the Son of David to "cleanse Jerusalem from the Gentiles" (*Ps. Sol.* 17:24). Jesus wanted it cleansed *for* the Gentiles.

Matthew 10:34-35

> "You must not think that I have come to bring peace to the earth;
> I have not come to bring peace, but a sword. I have come to set a
> man against his father, a daughter against her mother, a young
> wife against her mother-in-law; and a man will find his enemies
> under his own roof."

These verses have nothing to do with war.

(a) The illustrations show that the "sword" is a vivid metaphor for
division. Luke in the corresponding passages writes "division" (*Lk.*
12:51), and Macgregor usefully cites *Hebrews* 4:12: "For the word of
God is alive and active. It cuts more keenly than any two-edged sword,
piercing as far as the place where life and spirit, joints and marrow,
divide." So the word of God cleaves through a man's soul and cuts off
the genuine from the sham; so it cleaves through society and cuts off the
genuine from the sham.

(b) The form of phrase is ironic, according to a common enough
Semitic idiom, by which a consequence is expressed as if it were a
purpose. Jesus is not saying "The *purpose* of my coming is to split
families" but "The *result* of my coming is to split families." This is why
the passage goes on to say "No man is worthy of me who cares more for
father or mother than for me": the fifth commandment must give way
to the first. The truth here expressed is admirably dramatized in
Charles Sheldon's still fine novel *In His Steps.* In a society where the
family ties are more meaningful than in our loose Western
culture—Africa for instance—the conflict is even more poignant.

Luke 22:36-38

> "It is different now," he said; "whoever has a purse had better take
> it with him, and his pack too; and if he has no sword, let him sell
> his cloak to buy one. For Scripture says, 'And he was counted
> among the outlaws,' and these words, I tell you, must find
> fulfillment in me; indeed, all that is written of me is being
> fulfilled." "Look, Lord," they said, "we have two swords here."
> "Enough, enough!" he replied.

This is undoubtedly the most difficult passage in the New

Testament to reconcile with the general tenor of Jesus's teaching of nonviolent love. "See!" said the German theologian Spitta in 1915. "Jesus has summoned his followers to armed defense! He was no tender pacifist." Yet something seems wrong somewhere. As Johannes Weiss put it: "The martial note in this word is in direct contradiction to many others which definitely forbid resistance. It is in direct opposition to the whole spirit of primitive Christianity." So J.M. Creed: "It is unlikely that Jesus seriously entertained the thought of armed resistance, which indeed would be in conflict with the whole tenor of His life and teaching." So F.C. Burkitt: "It is impossible to believe that the command to buy a sword was meant literally or seriously." These commentators were not themselves pacifists.

(a) We ought to mention Professor S.G.F. Brandon's view that this verse is authentic and everything which points in the opposite direction an invention by the church of mollify the Roman authorities. Brandon would make Jesus a militarist, the church fifty years later pacifist.

(i) This really will not do. We have to take the evidence on its merits. We cannot reject the central core because of a peripheral puzzle.

(ii) Brandon's view supposes an extraordinary central control of documents which simply did not exist. The evidence suggests that the gospels were written in very different places, and that there was no such central authority.

(iii) It would argue extraordinary ineptitude on the part of the church to suggest that they could not see the implications of this saying when they were altering all the others.

(iv) As we have seen, the Form-Critics have argued that we cannot effectively get behind the evidence of the church. I do not myself agree with this, because I believe that the evidence of the church reflects a tradition which goes back to Jesus. But it would be temerarious to reject the evidence of the church and attribute something quite different to Jesus.

(b) It is quite impossible to accept the episode as an authentic conversation of Jesus in its literal meaning. Jesus is about to go to Gethsemane. When he is arrested he rebukes his follower who uses a sword (*Lk.* 22:49-51). He cannot therefore just beforehand have commanded them to carry swords for this purpose, when he rebukes them for the use of the sword. The rebuke in *Matthew* (*Mt.* 26:52) is stronger and fuller, and I have discussed it elsewhere.

(c) It is important to realize that to carry a sword was not necessarily a commitment to war.

(i) It would be normal practice in areas beyond the control of authority to carry a sword as protection against brigands and bandits. On the whole this would not seem to accord with the normal practice of Jesus, but some of the disciples might have had a sword for the journey from Galilee to Jerusalem.

(ii) It would also be normal practice to carry a sword as protection against wild animals, and there is no special reason to think that Jesus would disapprove of this. Candido Rondon, the extraordinary Brazilian who transformed the section of the Brazilian army charged with campaigning against the Indians into the Indian Protective Service, and whose work is one of the supreme examples of nonviolence in action, gave his men the rigid rule in their dealings with Indians: "Die if you need to; but kill never." But he allowed his men to carry guns against wild animals.

(d) We are still left with two explanations of Jesus's words. One is that they are not authentic. We note that these verses appear in *Luke* alone. He likes to whitewash the disciples; he may be trying to justify the use of swords in Gethsemane. Or something somewhere may have gone wrong with the tradition. But we must be very chary of rejecting the tradition. This sort of explanation savors too much of Brandon's methods.

(e) The alternative is that the words are not to be taken literally but metaphorically. According to this interpretation Jesus is issuing a general warning of crisis. It is, says William Barclay, "a vivid eastern way of telling the disciples that their very lives are at stake." A modern pacifist leader might well say "Now is the time to trust in God and keep your powder dry" or even "Up, guards, and at 'em" without speaking of *armed* resistance. According to this interpretation the disciples take the metaphor literally. This is supported by Jesus's response, well translated by NEB "Enough, enough!"; it is a common Semitic idiom, corresponding to something like our modern "Oh, for heaven's sake—!"

George Caird writes well: "The story of the upper room ends with a conversation which shows how deep was the gulf of misunderstanding which still separated the disciples from Jesus. He begins by reminding them (in words drawn from the mission charge to the seventy) of the halcyon days of the Galilean mission, when they were able to go out on their missionary tours relying wholly on hospitality for their maintenance. Now times have changed: Jesus is about to be executed as a criminal, and they, as the criminal's accomplices, will find every man's hand against them. The instruction to sell their coats and buy swords is an example of Jesus's fondness for violent metaphor (cf. *Matt.* 23:27; *Mark* 10:25), but the disciples take it literally, as pedants have continued to do every since. The words "*It is enough*" indicate, not satisfaction with the disciples' military preparedness, but a sad dismissal of the subject (cf. 1 *Kings* 19:4; *Mark* 14:41)."

Luke 7:5-10

"He deserves this favor from you," they said, "for he is a friend of our nation and it is he who built us our synagogue." Jesus went with them; but when he was not far from the house, the centurion sent friends with this message: "Do not trouble further, sir; it is not for me to have you under my roof, and that is why I did not presume to approach you in person. But say the word and my servant will be cured. I know, for in my position I am myself under orders, with soldiers under me. I say to one, 'go,' and he goes; to another, 'Come here,' and he comes; and to my servant, 'Do this,' and he does it." When Jesus heard this, he admired the man, and, turning to the crowd that was following him, he said, "I tell you, nowhere, even in Israel, have I found faith like this." And the messengers returned to the house and found the servant in good health.

It has occasionally been suggested that Jesus's commendation of the centurion's faith was incompatible with disapproval of the centurion's profession. The argument carries no weight.

(a) It is important to ask of any story, as of any parable, what is its point and beware of pressing features which do not pertain strictly to that point. Just as in the parable of the importunate widow we are not to suppose that God is like an unjust judge (*Lk.* 18:1-8), so here the point of the story is in the "pronouncement" associated with it. The rest is irrelevant to the purpose of the church in preserving the story.

(b) Jesus commends the faith of a prostitute (*Lk.* 7:36-50), of a superintendent of taxes (*Lk.* 19:1-10), and no doubt of numerous slave-owners. This does not imply approval of prostitution, graft and slavery. On the contrary it is typical of Jesus to approach people through their good points. A simple parallel. We may really believe that capitalism is evil, but that need not prevent our applauding the honesty or courage or devotion of an individual capitalist.

(c) The point has been sometimes made that for long periods the Roman soldiers were more of a police force than an army. The point is an entirely valid one, but should not be taken too far. In the course of police duties they were not afraid to kill.

(d) More important is the refusal of Christians to join the armed forces. We have seen that we must interpret the New Testament in the context of the church as well as in the context of Jesus's life. The church could not have interpreted and did not interpret this passage as upholding the military profession, since for nearly three hundred years there is no evidence of Christians joining the army, there is evidence that soldiers who were converted to Christianity could not become full church members until they had ceased to be soldiers, and the aspect of the soldier's profession which was primarily repugnant to Christians was the bloodshed with idolatry as an additional stumbling-block.

Mark 12:13-17

> A number of Pharisees and men of Herod's party were sent to trap him with a question. They came and said, "Master, you are an honest man, we know, and truckle to no man, whoever he may be; you teach in all honesty the way of life that God requires. Are we or are we not permitted to pay taxes to the Roman Emperor? Shall we pay or not?" He saw how crafty their question was, and said, "Why are you trying to catch me out? Fetch me a silver piece, and let me look at it." They brought one, and he said to them, "Whose head is this, and whose inscription?" "Caesar's," they replied. Then Jesus said, "Pay Caesar what is due to Caesar, and pay God what is due to God." And they heard him with astonishment.

(a) Some critics of pacifism have suggested that "Pay to Caesar what is due Caesar" means "If the government declares war and imposes conscription, go and fight." Merely to spell this out is to show an unbridged gulf.

(b) It is doubtful how much we ought to build on this passage. A trap-question receives an answer in kind. This is not, or not necessarily, a philosophy of life.

(c) Not merely so. The gospel-writers suggest that while in Jerusalem Jesus was teaching in the temple-precincts (cf. *Lk.* 20:1). To carry a coin with the head of the emperor Tiberius on it into those precincts was itself an offense against Jewish law. The moment one of Jesus's questioners produced the coin within the temple they were caught. They were not paying God what was due to God, and their possession of a coin with the emperor's head with implicit acceptance of his authority. The coin was the coin presented for taxation; the inscription ran "Tiberius Caesar Augustus, son of the Divine Augustus" — this in Yahweh's temple-courts!

(d) Nonetheless we can take Jesus's answer seriously. In so doing we must remember that Caesar does not stand for constitutional democratic authority but totalitarian alien rule. The question is set in the context of a political situation as tense as that of Norway or France under Nazi occupation, and Jesus's answer is a refusal to go the way of the guerrillas who refused to pay tribute.

(e) The relation between the two parts of Jesus's answer cannot be dogmatically affirmed. The answer has been taken to mean that God's claims and Caesar's claims are on totally different levels, and cannot clash, that God's claims and Caesar's claims are on the same level but do not clash, that Caesar's claims are limited by God's claims, and (in practice, though few would defend this in theory) that God's claims are limited by Caesar's claims: in all these Caesar is identified with the state. It is not, however, to be forgotten that Jesus's words were used at his trial as evidence of his disloyalty to Rome (*Lk*. 23:2). It is not a Zealot answer; it is not a collaborationist answer either. Without being dogmatic it is just to say that the practice of the Christians in the first two and a half centuries supports the third view. They claimed to be loyal citizens of Rome, but could not let the obligations of citizenship lead them away from their higher loyalty to God: they could not connive at idolatry and the taking of life.

Matthew 11:12

"Ever since the coming of John the Baptist the kingdom of Heaven has been subjected to violence and violent men are seizing it."

Nobody knows what these words mean.

(a) They might mean something like "The Kingdom of God is sweeping on like a storm and only the vigorous can catch hold of it" (NEB alternative).

(b) They might mean something like "The Kingdom of God is an object of violence and the violent are seizing it by force" (NEB).

(c) If the second is the true meaning the violent may refer to Herod and all those who are trying to suppress the prophetic voice.

(d) Alternatively there may be a reference to the Zealots. In the explosive political atmosphere of Jesus's Palestine it seems likely that there is, though we cannot be certain—that is, even if there is a reference to men of violence at all.

(e) In any case we have no means of knowing whether the words as originally spoken implied praise or blame, approval or disapproval.

In view of all the uncertainties it is impossible to build anything on these words: they remain an enigma.

John 15:13

"There is no greater love than this, that a man should lay down his life for his friends."

Probably these words are today quoted less frequently against pacifists than in the period between the wars, when they were set on numerous war memorials.

(a) It would be very wrong for those who for reasons of conscience said No to fighting, and who in consequence often led a sheltered and unendangered life, to disparage in any way the courage and suffering of those who, freely or under conscription, were in the battle-lines, or the agony of those whose loved ones were killed. Pacifists who claim to change the world by suffering have sometimes seemed distant from the suffering they profess, and can only be humble.

(b) Nonetheless, the job of the soldier is not to be killed, but to kill, and it is sentimental to ignore this fact. Jesus does *not* say: "There is no greater love than this, that a man should take the life of others for his friends." The challenge of love is to be willing to die for enemies rather than kill them. "Christ died for us while we were yet sinners, and that is God's own proof of his love towards us." (*Rom.* 5:8) "When we were God's enemies, we were reconciled to him through the death of his Son." (*Rom.* 5:10)

(c) It is frankly blasphemous to equate what a soldier is expected to do with Jesus's deliberate and freely chosen decision to be crucified rather than use evil means to establish the kingdom. Sir John Arkwright's hymn "O Valiant Hearts" (still in *Hymns Ancient and Modern*), suggesting that "Christ, our Redeemer, went the selfsame way" as the soldier, and that the fallen soldier has offered a lesser Calvary, is a misuse of words. Erasmus wrote, "The Cross is the banner and standard of him who has overcome and triumphed, not by fighting and slaying, but by his own bitter death. With the Cross do you deprive of life your brother, whose life was rescued by the Cross?"

Romans 1:19-21

For all that may be known of God by men lies plain before their eyes; indeed God himself has disclosed it to them. His invisible attributes, that is to say his everlasting power and deity, have been visible, ever since the world began, to the eye of reason, in the things he has made. There is therefore no possible defense for their conduct; knowing God, they have refused to honor him as God, or to render him thanks. Hence all their thinking has ended in futility, and their misguided minds are plunged in darkness.

Romans 2:14-15

While Gentiles who do not possess the law carry out its precepts by the light of nature, then, although they have no law, they are their own law, for they display the effect of the law inscribed on their hearts. Their conscience is called as witness, and their own thoughts argue the case on either side, against them or even for them, on the day when God judges the secrets of human hearts through Christ Jesus.

These are two classic texts in which the Catholic church has found scriptural justification for a doctrine of natural law: out of this church authority derived the doctrine of the "just" war.

(a) The first of these passages must be interpreted in the light of the second.

(b) In an important article "Natural Law in the New Testament" in the American journal *Biblical Research* (9, 1964, 3-13) a Catholic writer, Father John McKenzie, has shown that when Paul speaks of law he is not speaking of the Stoic *lex naturae* ("natural law"), but of the Torah, the Mosaic Law: the NEB translation in fact makes the point very clearly.

(c) Paul never regards the light of nature among the Gentiles, or the Mosaic Law among the Jews, as anything more than a historical preparation for the gospel which is superseded by the gospel. There is no New Testament justification for suggesting that the Christian should live in any other way than is revealed in Christ. So Father Josef Fuchs wrote in *Natural Law: A Theological Investigation* (p. 175), "The meaning of the natural law is love." So Father McKenzie rightly expounded Paul, "I think that Paul would say that Jesus did not live and die in order that men might live by a morality of reason and nature. This they had already."

(d) The classic doctrine of the just war has been most recently and sympathetically expounded by the American Protestant theologian Paul Ramsey in his book *War and the Christian Conscience* and his pamphlet

The Limits of Nuclear War. Ramsey admits the pacifism of the early church but suggests that the change from pacifism to a just-war position was a change of tactics not of principle. This cannot be sustained. As we shall see in the next chapter the factors which stopped Christians from fighting for nearly three centuries were still valid when Christians were in positions of political responsibility.

(e) The tragic fact is that the just war is a peculiarly elastic doctrine. Ramsey argues for discrimination and limitation. He argues for a discriminate slaughter of 25,000,000 as being legitimately Christian where an indiscriminate slaughter of 215,000,000 would be unchristian. He knows well that those who across the ages formulated the doctrine of the just war would have regarded the "discriminate slaughter of 25,000,000" as mass murder.

(f) The traditional marks of the just war were something as follows. First, the cause must be just. We know enough about politics to know that a cause is seldom just in an absolute sense, that the ordinary soldier or citizen has no chance of knowing whether it is just, that both sides argue sincerely that their cause is just, and that anyone in a "Christian" country who thought that "justice" was the "other" side and acted accordingly would be shot. Second, the means must be just. This used to be taken to imply that they should not involve the death of innocent people. Apart from the fact that the conscript soldier can hardly be held to be guilty, we know that modern warfare, however discriminate, cannot avoid the death of the innocent. Further, a just war should not involve excessive destructive power. No ancient theologian would have accounted modern war justifiable on these grounds. Third, there must be a reasonable expectation of a just result. This is now impossible. If the church were true to the traditional sub-christian doctrine of the just war, all future war would be proscribed. War can never again be "just" as the church defined "just."

(g) But the doctrine of the just war is sub-christian. There is no New Testament justification for a doctrine which substitutes natural law for the way of Christ. If there is any doctrine of natural law in these passages, it is that some Gentiles have lived according to the Mosaic Law without having heard the Mosaic Law. That is all. It is nowhere suggested that Stoic ethics are valid for the Christian. Jesus shows, to Jews and Gentiles alike, a new way.

Luke 11:21-22

"When a strong man fully armed is on guard over his castle his possessions are safe. But when someone stronger comes upon him and overpowers him, he carries off the arms and armor on which the man had relied and divides the plunder."

(a) The quotation of proof-texts for any aspect of Christianity is a dubious procedure; the citation of phrases out of context is intolerable. Archbishop Whately once said of a curate who erred in this way: "I should like to hear that young man preach on the text 'Hang all the law and the prophets!' " Something similar happens over these words. The first verse is quoted out of context as a justification of defensive armaments. In fact if we look at the whole passage its implications are the exact opposite. There is no security in arms; it is illusory.

(b) But in fact nothing can be built on this at all. The words are parabolic. Jesus is not speaking of war or the private bearing of arms; he is using an illustrative parallel to illuminate some point now lost. If we accept the context which Luke gives to the words then he is simply saying, "Satan may look impregnable, but the power of God in me is shattering his citadel."

Matthew 22:7

The king was furious; he sent troops to kill those murderers and set their town on fire.

It is hardly worth mentioning this and other passages from the parables; except that they still cause difficulty to some.

(a) In the parables Jesus shows life as it is, not as it should be. He portrays an unjust judge; he does not suggest that judges should be unjust. He portrays a violent and brutal king; he does not suggest that those responsible for political decisions should be violent and brutal.

(b) It is essential in interpreting the parables to take the point of the parable; the rest is vivid color to add verisimilitude to a narrative which might otherwise be bald and unconvincing. The Jewish rabbi liked to make his point in the form of a story, and Jesus was an exceptionally brilliant exponent of the art. But the point, so to speak, is the point. Thus Jesus tells a story of an importunate widow and an unjust judge. According to Luke the point of the story is constancy in prayer. If we pressed the details God might appear as an unjust judge! This is not Jesus's intention.

THE WARFARE OF CHRIST

Mark 13:7-13

"When you hear the noise of battle near at hand and the news of battles far away, do not be alarmed. Such things are bound to happen; but the end is still to come. For nation will make war upon nation, kingdom upon kingdom; there will be earthquakes in many places; there will be famines. With these things the birth-pangs of the new age begin.

"As for you, be on your guard. You will be handed over to the courts. You will be flogged in synagogues. You will be summoned to appear before governors and kings on my account to testify in their presence. But before the end the Gospel must be proclaimed to all nations. So when you are arrested and taken away, do not worry beforehand about what you will say, but when the time comes say whatever is given you to say; for it will not be you that speak, but the Holy Spirit. Brother will betray brother to death, and the father his child; children will turn against their parents and send them to their death. All will hate you for your allegiance to me; but the man who holds out to the end will be saved."

Most of us, pacifist or non-pacifist, if we are honest, find the apocalyptic chapters of the New Testament somewhat disconcerting. Here it will be enough to say four things.

(a) This is one of the comparatively few passages where prophecy in the Hebrew sense of forth-telling the word of God blends into prophecy in the popular sense of fore-telling the future. Many scholars would say that the corresponding passages in *Matthew* and *Luke* are, so to speak "prophecies after the event," and contain elements descriptive of the Jewish War of A.D. 66-70 and the fall of Jerusalem, put back into the mouth of Jesus. Certainly Mark's readers would read it with reference to the persecutions they themselves knew, when they were hated "because of the Name." There is in fact nothing here that a politically sensitive person could not have foretold. It is sadly true that the noise of battle did ring out, and nations did war with nations, kingdoms with kingdoms, and have been doing so ever since.

(b) To say that a thing is going to happen is not to approve of it. Jesus no more approved of these wars than of the earthquakes and famines which he similarly predicted.

(c) The very words are to be seen against the background of the prophecy found in both *Isaiah* (2:4) and *Micah* (4:3), that in the Messianic age "nation shall not lift up sword against nation." Part of the witness of the gospels is that for those who have accepted Jesus as their Lord the kingdom has in some sense already come (cf. *Lk.* 17:20-21); they are living in the new age and are to continue to live by the new covenant of nonviolent love.

(d) Hence it is quite clear that the Christian disciples are not envisaged as taking part in these wars. They are not called to fight but to suffer. They must keep their allegiance to Jesus, and that, as is elsewhere pellucid, means living out the way of love. "Not everyone who calls me 'Lord, Lord' will enter the kingdom of heaven, but only those who do the will of my heavenly Father" (*Mt.* 7:21). The parable of the sheep and the goats is ample commentary on the theme (*Mt.* 25:31-36). It is the man who holds out to the end in allegience to Jesus, in love, in suffering, who will be saved.

Ephesians 6:10-17

> Finally then, find your strength in the Lord, in his mighty power. Put on all the armor which God provides, so that you may be able to stand firm against the devices of the devil. For our fight is not against human foes, but against cosmic power, against the authorities and potentates of this dark world, against the super-human forces of evil in the heavens. Therefore, take up God's armor; then you will be able to stand your ground when things are at their worst, to complete every task and still to stand. Stand firm, I say. Buckle on the belt of truth; for coat of mail put on integrity; let the shoes on your feet be the gospel of peace, to give you firm footing; and, with all these, take up the great shield of faith, with which you will be able to quench all the flaming arrows of the evil one. Take salvation for helmet; for sword, take that which the Spirit gives you — the words that come from God.

There is no need to pursue this passage at length. This is the *militia Christi*, the service in Christ's army. So far from having any connection with military service, it is incompatible with it. "I threw down my arms," said Marcellus, a third-century soldier convert, "for it was not seemly that a Christian man, who renders military service to the Lord Christ, should render it by earthly injuries." "The soldiers of Christ," said Ambrose in his speech against Auxentius, "require neither arms nor spears of iron." Pope Nicholas I (858-867) went further: "The soldiers of the world are distinct from the soldiers of the church. Hence it is improper for the soldiers of the church to fight for the affairs of the world, which involves them inevitably in the spilling of blood." That is unequivocal.

The passage in fact *contrasts* the behavior of the soldier and of the Christian. Our fight is not against human foes. Henry Child Carter, in a hymn based on this very passage, puts the point clearly:

> Give me to see the foes that I must fight,
>> Powers of the darkness, throned where Thou shouldst reign,
> Read the directions of Thy wrath aright,
>> Lest, striking flesh and blood, I strike in vain.

"The weapons of the gospel," said the Roman Catholic Christopher Butler (then Abbot of Downside) at the Vatican Council "are not nuclear but spiritual; it wins its victories not by war but by suffering." What Paul is seeking is precisely what William James called "the moral equivalent of war."

John 18:36

> Jesus replied, "My kingdom does not belong to this world. If it did, my followers would be fighting to save me from arrest by the Jews."

It is quite extraordinary that this passage has been quoted in defense of war.

(a) Those who do so quote it usually finish the quotation at "fighting." (AV "If my kingdom were of this world, then would my servants fight...") In so doing they make it a general statement rather than a particular one. Jesus is establishing a Messianic kingdom of a new and special sort. He is not leading a violent resistance movement to set himself on a throne. He will reign, but from the cross; he finds his kingdom in nonviolent suffering.

(b) Even if we were to generalize it would be only as a statement of fact, not of approval. "In the world kings lord it over their subjects... *Not so with you*" (*Lk.* 22:25-26). Luther claimed on the basis of this passage that a war waged by an accredited sovereign for just ends had the *imprimatur* of Jesus. There is in fact no generalized statement, and no approval.

(c) [1]On the contrary what the passage says is that Christ's kingdom does *not* belong to this world, and that is why his followers are *not* fighting to save him. This is the kingdom to which all Christian disciples owe their primary allegiance.

(d) We may legitimately think that Paul's account of the *militia Christi* in *Ephesians* 6:10-17, which we have just discussed, in an expansion, and an entirely legitimate expansion of this passage.

(e) Of course this may involve a Christian in conflict with the state. This can happen at any time, and it can happen over much more than war. No man can serve two masters, and there are times when we have to choose between God and the state.

(f) The choice can again be exemplified from a third-century soldier convert named Tarachus, who declared simply, "Because I was a Christian I have now chosen to be a civilian," from the same speech of Ambrose in which he declared, "The servants of God do not rely for their protection on material defenses but on the divine Providence," and from the Synod of Ratisbon in 742 which decreed, "We absolutely and in all circumstances forbid all God's servants to carry arms, to fight, and to march against an army or against an enemy." We cannot, as they did, limit God's servants to the clergy; their understanding of the gospel was clear and true.

Revelation 12:7-9

> Then war broke out in heaven. Michael and his angels waged war upon the dragon. The dragon and his angels fought, but they had not the strength to win, and no foothold was left them in heaven. So the great dragon was thrown down, that serpent of old that led the whole world astray, whose name is Satan, or the Devil—thrown down to the earth, and his angels with him.

Revelation is by any standards a difficult book. Macgregor quotes a letter to the *British Weekly* on August 30th, 1934 which ran, "I would very much like to know what justification writers have for their extreme pacifist views. Whether we wish it or not, we still have the Battle of Armageddon to face. Will these friends then, when the great battle of Christ's forces against anti-Christ takes place, be pacifists?" Perhaps we might exemplify a similar point of view by C.S. Lewis's novel *Voyage to Venus* in which the repulsion of spiritual evil is achieved through physical combat. To this we may say three things.

(a) There was a tendency in the 1920s and 1930s to take the apocalyptic books of the Bible and the apocalyptic elements in the New

Testament insufficiently seriously, and Macgregor in his day succumbed to that temptation. Nonetheless he was surely right to warn us "against fantastically literal interpretations." We are dealing with the language of images, of poetry, of myth projected forwards instead of backwards. The language conveys to us truths through picture-language. It is ultimately the truths not the pictures which matter.

(b) *Revelation* is about warfare in heaven not on earth. H. Windisch in his book *Der Messianische Krieg und das Urchristentum* (Tubingen 1909) wrote well: "Heavenly beings and superhuman heavenly powers alone wage war on God's behalf. When men fight, they are doomed to destruction; only the devil lets men fight for him. The fighters whom God blesses cannot be men" (p. 76).

(c) *Revelation* must be set in context within the New Testament, and interpreted in the light of the words of Jesus and of Paul which we have just been examining. The passage from *Ephesians* is especially relevant, for Paul is there writing of the fight against cosmic powers and the superhuman forces of evil. And the weapons are no physical weapons, and we notice that they include the shoes of the gospel of peace.

THE WIDER WITNESS

1 *Corinthians* 1:13

Surely Christ has not been divided among you!

So the NEB with ponderous precision; the AV's "Is Christ divided?" has more power, and is not seriously misleading.

(a) The Fellowship of Reconciliation began effectively in July 1914 when a British Quaker, Henry Hodgkin, and a German Lutheran, Friedrich Siegmund-Schultze, knowing that war was imminent, shook hands at Cologne railway station with the words "We are one in Christ and can never be at war." The experience of fellowship in Christ led them to repudiate war.

(b) Professor John Hick in his remarkable contribution to my *Studies in Christian Social Commitment* (Independent Press 1954), after examining with sympathy the problem of the individual conscience, urges that the tolerance of war by Christians makes nonsense of the ecumenical movement. "Is the internal peace of the Body of Christ to be merely a dependent reflection of the degree of political amity prevailing in the world at a given time? Is the unity of the World Council of Churches to be merely a shadow of the precarious unity of the United Nations? If so, Christianity is in the last resort a world-religion only by courtesy of, and in proportion to, the momentary success of men's political contrivings.... Indeed it is difficult to conceive a more effective reversal for the cause of Christ than that after nearly two thousand years of Christian history His committed disciples should engage in fratricidal conflict with one another, their distinctive way of life and mutual relationship being thereby abandoned or suspended. If the Christian revelation is true, there can be no power of evil strong enough to compel Christian people, united in faith to their one Lord, to wage war upon one another and so to crucify afresh the Christ whose Body they are" (p. 35).

Galatians 3:28

> There is no such thing as Jew and Greek, slave and freeman, male and female; for you are all one person in Christ Jesus.

Colossians 3:11

> There is no question here of Greek and Jew, circumcised and uncircumcised, barbarian, Scythian, freeman, slave; but Christ is all, and is in all.

In these two passages Paul spells out more clearly the *transvaluation* worked by Christ. Paul takes the three most fundamental divisions, nation or race, social class, and sex, and claims that Christ has broken down the barriers and broken through the distinctions. Charles Wesley puts it magnificently in one of his hymns:

> Love, like death, hath all destroyed,
> Rendered all distinctions void;
> Names, and sects, and parties fall:
> Thou, O Christ, art all in all.

There is an old Jewish prayer which Paul must have used every morning before his conversion, a prayer of thanks to God that "Thou has not made me a Gentile, a slave or a woman." We sometimes underestimate the change in Paul and others like him. We must think of a leading exponent of *apartheid*, a man of strong class-consciousness, an invincibly arrogant male. The change is the mark of the Christian revolution.

(a) The world to which Christ came was man-dominated. Women took a back seat. Jesus startled others by the freedom of his conversation with women (e.g. *Jn*. 4 : 27) ; he treated women as his fellows. In a society of that sort men sow their wild oats, women become culpably damaged goods. In the precious story of the woman taken in adultery (*Jn.* 8 : 1-11) Jesus refuses to let the men get away with this dual standard of morality; they must apply the same standard to the woman and to themselves. Women were prominent in the early church: witness Mary (the mother of John Mark) , Phoebe, Nympha, Prisca and others. The freedom of encounter scandalized and was misunderstood by the pagans, but it was a real breakthrough in human relations, though later the traditional dominance of the male was restored. The work of Christ has not yet had its fulfillment. But for those who are in Christ a fellow-Christian is a fellow-Christian, male or female: we are one in Christ.

(b) This is easy to see, less easy to realize. The same revolution takes place between people of different nationalities. Again the British and the German pastor come to mind. Paul takes as example two of the most exclusive groups — the Jews, to whom all other peoples were Gentiles, lesser breeds without the law, and the Greeks, to whom all other peoples were barbarians, uncultured savages who could only say "bar-bar-bar." Christ breaks down these barriers so that they become irrelevant.

But we are not to suppose that the revolution is to be confined within the church. On the contrary, it is the Christians' calling to shine like stars in a dark world and proffer the word of life (*Phil.* 2 : 16) . In other words, for the Christian the barriers are already broken within the church, and he must play his part in breaking them down outside the church.

A Christian cannot be a nationalist. If we are in Christ there is no such thing as "Jew and Greek"; if there is for us a division between "Jew and Greek" then we are not in Christ. Nationalism has been a, perhaps the, major cause of war. It is for the Christian to cut out the effect by cutting at the root.

(c) So too in Christ economic and social distinctions are done away. He held a common purse with his disciples. The natural effect of the power of the Holy Spirit on the first Christians was that everything was held in common (*Acts* 4 : 32) . Here too we shall cut away the causes of war if we are in Christ. There will not be peace on earth as long as there are those who are hungry and are not fed, as long as the world is divided between overprivileged and underprivileged.

2 *Corinthians* 5:18-20

> From first to last this has been the work of God. He has reconciled us men to himself through Christ, and he has enlisted us in this service of reconciliation. What I mean is, that God was in Christ reconciling the world to himself, no longer holding men's misdeeds against them, and that he has entrusted us with the message of reconciliation. We come therefore as Christ's ambassadors.

These words have been the inspiration of the Fellowship of Reconciliation; the very name of the Fellowship reflects them.
(a) Curiously enough, the Christian pacifist movement has tended to misinterpret them. On the face of it they entrust the Christian disciple not with the mission of reconciling man with man, but with the mission of reconciling man with God. This is an important enough ministry, a vital and essential one, but it is not the ministry of reconciling the nations. Should we therefore cease to use it in that context?
(b) Plainly not, for it is impossible to reconcile men with God and leave them unreconciled with one another. If a man does not love his brother whom he has seen how can he love God whom he has not seen? (1 *Jn.* 4:20). Our love of God is expressed through love of the neighbor.
(c) In fact the ministry of reconciliation among men is clear through the New Testament from the Beatitudes onwards.

1 *Peter* 2:13-17

> Submit yourself to every human institution for the sake of the Lord, whether to the sovereign as supreme or to the governor as his deputy for the punishment of criminals and the commendation of those who do right. For it is the will of God that by your good conduct you should put ignorance and stupidity to silence.
>
> Live as free men; not however as though your freedom were to provide a screen for wrongdoing, but as slaves in God's service. Give due honor to everyone: love to the brotherhood, reverence to God, honor to the sovereign.

This is Peter's version of the "Pay to Caesar" tradition (*Mk.* 12:13-17) and Paul's instruction to submit to the supreme authorities (*Rom.* 13:1): the word "sovereign" would be better "emperor." The tradition is the same.

(a) The Christian is not an anarchist; an ordered society is God's will for the world. The Christian is a loyal citizen. If this is true under an authoritarian regime, how much more so when the Christian can participate in the decision-making processes.

(b) The Christian is a better citizen of this world than others; he shows them up by his good conduct.

(c) The Christian lives in the state as a free man; to God he owes absolute obedience. Peter knows of course—who better?—that Jesus called the disciples no longer slaves but friends. The language is vivid, and is intended to convey that God's claims are stronger than the state's. "It will, then, be true," says William Barclay, "that there may be times when the Christian will fulfill his highest duty and obligation to the state by refusing to obey the state, and by insisting on obeying God; for, by so doing, at least he can witness to the truth, and at best he can even compel the state to take the Christian way."

Philippians 3:20

We, by contrast, are citizens of heaven.

The idea here is a very interesting one. From the eighth century B.C. the Greek cities began to settle colonies round the Mediterranean. Each of these would take the constitution, laws, organization and customs of the mother-city. They might be surrounded with people of vastly different traditions, and inclinations, but they maintained their primary loyalty. This, says Paul, is the state of Christians in the world. We are a colony of heaven. That is our commonwealth. There is our citizenship. And this is how we should live. We live out our citizenship of heaven on earth and that, not worldly wisdom, should determine our way of life. The kingdom of heaven is among us: we live as a colony of the kingdom. And if an earthly state decrees war and the way of God's kingdom decrees nonviolent love, it is to nonviolent love that we are called.

Romans 12:2

Adapt yourselves no longer to the pattern of this present world, but let your minds be remade and your whole nature thus transformed. Then you will be able to discern the will of God, and to know what is good, acceptable, and perfect.

2 Corinthians 5:17

> When anyone is united to Christ, there is a new world; the old
> order has gone, and a new order has already begun.

(a) It is right to stress these words, for there are so many who admit the
Holy Spirit on condition that he alters nothing, and whose Christian
commitment, as Sorokin remarked of some converts he studied, alters
their verbal patterns not their social behavior. And who bothers to
crucify us?

The true Christian is a revolutionary. He seeks to turn the world
upside-down (*Acts* 17:6 AV). We ought to be suspicious of our
Christian commitment if we find ourselves too easily acquiescing in the
status quo and at one with the Establishment. In an important article in
The Scottish Journal of Theology for June 1968 the Czech theologian,
J.M. Lochman, wrote well:

"At the same time, however, the 'pacifist' is warned: the testimony
of nonviolent love is not true if it is understood quietistically or
ideologically (as a luxury-attitude in which the *beati possidentes* can
indulge) ; it is true only if it is expressed in serious Christian testimony,
i.e. in a revolutionary way, attacking the inhuman, godless structures of
the world in the light of God's kingdom. It is only through ecumenical
solidarity with the hungry, oppressed people in the developing
countries, and by supporting their justified revolutionary demands, that
the privileged Christians of Europe today can make a testimony of
nonviolent love which will carry any conviction."

(b) The means of the revolution are nonviolent. In fact the Christian
lives his life in the new age and the new order. He lives a life of sharing,
he lives peace.

(c) War is part of the old order not of the new. Those theologians who
try to persuade Christians not to take the pacifist commitment are — not
to mince words — persuading them to adapt themselves to the pattern of
this present world. But (the AV though a shade less precise is more
incisive, as so often) we are not to be conformed to this world, we are to
be transformed; and in being transformed ourselves we are to transform
the world.

Matthew 25:31-46

> "When the Son of Man comes in his glory and all the angels with
> him, he will sit in state on his throne, with all the nations gathered

before him. He will separate men into two groups, as a shepherd separates the sheep from the goats, and he will place the sheep on his right hand and the goats on his left. Then the king will say to those on his right hand, 'You have my Father's blessing; come, enter and possess the kingdom that has been ready for you since the world was made. For when I was hungry, you gave me food; when thirsty you gave me drink; when I was a stranger you took me into your home, when naked you clothed me; when I was ill you came to my help, when in prison you visited me.' Then the righteous will reply, 'Lord, when was it that we saw you hungry and fed you, or thirsty and gave you drink, a stranger and took you home, or naked and clothed you? When did we see you ill or in prison, and come to visit you?' And the king will answer, 'I tell you this: anything you did for one of my brothers here, however humble, you did for me.' Then he will say to those on his left hand, 'The curse is upon you; go from my sight to the eternal fire that is ready for the devil and his angels. For when I was hungry you gave me nothing to eat, when thirsty nothing to drink; when I was a stranger you gave me no home, when naked you did not clothe me; when I was ill and in prison you did not come to my help.' And they too will reply, 'Lord, when was it that we saw you hungry or thirsty or a stranger or naked or ill or in prison, and did nothing for you?' And he will answer, 'I tell you this: anything you did not do for one of these, however humble, you did not do for me.' And they will go away to eternal punishment, but the righteous will enter eternal life."

This is the most solemn of all the parables of Jesus. "I remember," said Dr. Johnson, "that my Maker has said that he will place the sheep on his right hand and the goats on his left." We bring it in here for cogent and sufficient reasons.

(a) It is a judgment of the nations, not of individuals.

(b) The nations are condemned for failing to feed the hungry and care for the needy. Probably two-thirds of mankind are hungry today; about half are said to be starving.

(c) The world expenditure on armaments in 1970 was calculated at two billion dollars a year and rising by 6 per cent each year. Now reread the parable. By that judgment we in the Western affluent world are living in hell, and shall be until be disarm and use our resources for the service of those in need. It is time that the so-called Christian nations took our Christianity seriously.

THE PACIFISM OF
THE EARLY CHURCH

THE PACIFISM OF THE EARLY CHURCH

It cannot be too strongly stated that the New Testament is a document of the church, and certainly contains material down to the very end of the first century A.D.; most scholars would say that some of the books date from the second century. But, this last apart, *Revelation* must be a full sixty years after the crucifixion, and few would date *Matthew* in its present form much less than fifty years after the crucifixion. The Form-critics have shown that the material out of which the gospels were built was preserved within the church for a variety of purposes. To deny that it goes back, or for the most part goes back, to Jesus seems to me abject folly, comparable with that of those who once denied the existence of Jesus altogether. Had there been no Jesus there would have been no church, and had Jesus not taught and lived out a way of life the church would have had no way of life. It follows therefore, and follows from the very solid consistency between epistles and gospels, that we are dealing with a way of life which was attributed to Jesus and accepted by Christians up to two or more generations after his death — on the evidence of the New Testament.

This is important.

(a) The New Testament does not comment upon the frontier wars fought by the Romans. From Tiberius to Nerva there were not in fact so many of them, and Britain, one of the main centers of fighting, must have been not even a name to many of the Christians of the eastern Mediterranean, though at Rome Pomponia Graecina, wife of Aulus Plautius, the conqueror of Britain, was accused of "foreign superstition," which suggests that she was a convert of Judaism or Christianity: if the latter it was a strange irony (Tacitus *Annals* 13, 32). Towards the end of the century it looks as if Christianity began to come near the seats of power. Flavius Clemens, one of the royal family, was condemned, again for depraved superstition. He is described as indifferent to the public welfare, which is exactly what would be said of a man whose religious scruples led him to withdraw from public positions (Seutonius *Domitian* 15, 1). These were exceptional. In general the picture of the first-century church is that drawn by Paul: "Few of you are men of wisdom, by any human standard; few are powerful or highly born" (1 *Cor.* 1:26). In relation to the wars of Rome, with one exception, Christians were far from the theater of fighting and even further from the offices where decisions were taken. (b) That exception was the Jewish revolt and Rome's suppression of it in A.D. 66-70. For all Paul's work we must not forget that a high proportion of Christians came out of the Jewish community, nor should we forget that Judaea shows Roman imperialism at its worst, brutal and covetous, altogether lacking that tactful concern for local custom which was a major explanation of the peaceful nature of Roman dominion elsewhere. This, from the Jewish view, was a war of liberation, every bit as much as the French *maquis* of 1940-44 or the South African guerrillas have seen themselves as liberators. The New Testament evidence of the Christian attitude is clear: it is explicit in *Matthew*, *Romans* and 1 *Peter*, and it is consistent throughout: we must remember that it was clear for years before that the explosion was coming and for years after that the last shot had not been fired. Love extends to enemies. That the Christians were not siding with the Romans against the Jews is seen in that they do identify the Romans as enemies and offer a different way of meeting them. All the instructions to submit to the emperor, the governor and the magistrates have to be seen in this context; they are an injunction to refrain from violent rebellion against Rome. There was a Christian community in Jerusalem at the time the city was beleaguered; they took a communal decision to leave and make for Pella in the Decapolis (Eusebius *History of the Church* 3, 5, 3). The historical statement has been doubted; they could not, it is suggested, have slipped through the Roman lines; but it is not easy to see how the tradition arose if it were not a true one. The pacifism of the church at this time is not in doubt. S.G.F. Brandon, whose curious attempt to make a violent revolutionary out of Jesus we have noticed, suggests that the very emphasis on pacifism is an attempt to put things right with Rome. The emphasis is certain.

(c) The very description of Flavius Clemens as indolent or indifferent to public affairs suggests a certain political quietism on the part of the Christians. To understand what this means we must look briefly at the structure of government under the Roman Empire. Whether at the center or in the municipalities all round the Mediterranean world the decisions were taken by a relatively small group of very rich men, who were expected to use their resources of wealth, skill and experience in the public interest. Christians simply were not in this group, and if any of this group were converted to Christianity the church and its charitable work had first claim on their work, and they withdrew from high office partly because their energies were elsewhere, and partly because high office involved them in actions which their consciences orbade, such as idolatry.

d) The bulk of the citizens bore little or no political power. But they could still participate in the life of the community. James Douglass, in his admirable *The Non-Violent Cross* (p. 192) has said, "It is just as false to read into the Gospel a withdrawal from the world's conflicts as it is to equate a whip of cords with a hydrogen bomb." Already we are seeing the claim which was proudly made later, that Christians are more loyal and active citizens, better members of the community than their fellows. In short the often-made statement that the Christians at this period were politically quietist is misleading unless it is qualified. In any modern sense 99 per cent of the inhabitants of the Empire were politically quietist because they were politically impotent, and rather more than 99 per cent of Christians belonged to that group. But, though one or two might contract out of positions of power, this did not prevent any of them from being effective citizens.

In the two centuries which followed there is a consistent pattern, but with an increasing tendency to accommodation with the world.

The central traditions of the church were uncompromisingly pacifist.

a) There is no writer who touches the subject who is not a pacifist.

(i) Justin Martyr, who won his title under Marcus Aurelius in 165, wrote a defense of Christianity to Antoninus Pius in about 138. In it he quotes the Old Testament prophecy

nation shall not lift sword against nation

nor ever again be trained for war. (*Is.* 2:44)

and goes on "You can be convinced that this has happened. . . . We who used to kill one another, do not make war on our enemies. We refuse to tell lies or deceive our inquisitors; we prefer to die acknowledging Christ" (1 *Apol.* 39). In another work, *The Dialogue with Trypho*, he writes similarly, after quoting the same prophecy, "We who were filled with war and mutual slaughter and all wickedness have each and all throughout the earth changed our instruments of war, our swords into ploughshares and our spears into farming-tools, and cultivate piety, justice, love of mankind, faith and the hope which we have from the Father through the Crucified One" (110).

(ii) Tatian, a Syrian convert of Justin, writing about 160, wrote, "I do not want to be an emperor; I do not want wealth; I refuse military office; I loathe sexual looseness" (*Discourse to the Greeks* 11), and again "You intend to make war and take Apollo as your adviser in murder" (19) ; there is a grim pun since Apollo might mean Destroyer.

(iii) Athenagoras wrote a defense of Christianity to Marcus

Aurelius in about 177, in which he explicitly says that Christians ma
not take life "even justly," and refuse to watch public executions o
gladiatorial fights. Human life is sacred to the Christian: "How coul
anyone accuse of murder and cannibalism men who, as they well know
cannot bear to see a man killed even if killed justly.... We, thinkin
that to watch a man being killed is practically equivalent to taking life
refuse to attend the gladiatorial displays" (*An Embassy about th
Christians* 35).

(iv) Iranaeus, a man who combined gentle spirit with decisiv
action, wrote of the revolution achieved among the Christians: "If th
law of liberty, that is the Word of God, proclaimed to the whole eart
by the apostles who went out from Jerusalem, has achieved a revolutio
of such magnitude that the very peoples have made their warlike lance
and swords into ploughs and changed them into sickles which he gav
for reaping corn, and now do not know how to fight, but when strucl
offer even the other cheek, the prophets made this declaration of no on
but him who accomplished it" (*Against Heresies,* 4, 56, 4).

(v) Clement of Alexandria, one of the sanest and most attractiv
of Christian writers, throughout his ample writings insists on th
Christian's rejection of war and commitment to peace. "We are bein
educated not in war but in peace" (*The Tutor* 1, 12, 98). "We are th
race given over to peace" (*ibid.* 2, 21, 32). "We have made use of onl
one instrument, the peaceful word, with which we do honor to God
(*ibid.* 4, 42). "We do not train women like Amazons to be manly i
war, since we wish even men to be peaceable" (*Miscellanies* 4, 8, 61)

(vi) Origen (185-254), Clement's student and successor, had on
of the most comprehensively magisterial intellects of all time, thoug
the Christian establishment of the time found some of his speculatio
too daring. His supreme work lay in Biblical scholarship, but his bes
known writing is probably his defense of Christianity called *Agains
Celsus*, in answer to an attack from a Platonic philosopher of tha
name. Part of Origen's defense affirms Christian pacifism, and for th
first time we have the question "What would happen if..." in this cas
"Rome disarmed?" and the answer of faith.

> The existence of many kingdoms would have been an obstacl
> to the extension of Jesus's teaching throughout the whole world, no
> only because of what has just been said, but also on account o
> people everywhere being compelled to bear arms and to make wa
> for their countries.... How would it have been possible for thi
> peaceable teaching, which does not even allow men to tak

vengeance on their enemies, to prevail, unless at the appearance of Jesus the world's affairs had changed everywhere into a gentler state? (2, 30)

If a revolt had been the cause of the Christians' combining, and if they had derived their origin from the Jews, to whom it was allowed to take arms on behalf of their families and to destroy their enemies, the Law-giver of the Christians would not have altogether forbidden the killing of a human being, teaching that violence done to a man on the part of his own disciples, however unrighteous that man may be, is never right — for he did not deem it becoming to his own Divine legislation to allow the killing of any man whatever. (3, 7)

To those who ask us where we have come from or who is our commander, we say that we have come in accordance with the counsels of Jesus to cut down our warlike and arrogant swords of dispute into ploughshares, and we convert into sickles the spears we used in fighting. For we no longer take a sword against a nation, nor do we learn any more to make war, having become sons of peace for the sake of Jesus, who is our commander. (5, 33)

If, according to Celsus' supposition, all the Romans were to be converted they will by praying overcome their enemies — or rather they will not make war at all, being guarded by the Divine power, which promised to save five whole cities for the sake of fifty righteous men. (8, 70)

(vii) Meantime in the Latin-speaking world and especially in Africa Christians were becoming articulate. The first great Christian Latin writer was Tertullian (c. 160-220) and he remains one of the greatest. He was converted by the example of martyrdom. He had a combative spirit, but a commitment to pacifism. In later life he became a Montanist, with an intense belief in the present power of the Holy Spirit, and stringent moral standards. His pacifism is consistent.

The Lord's capacity for suffering was wounded in Malchus, and so he cursed the works of the sword forever. (*On Patience* 3)

For what war should we not have been fit and ready, however outnumbered, we who face massacre so readily, were it not that in our way of life it is more permissible to suffer death than to inflict it. (*Apology* 37)

Is it right to occupy oneself with the sword, when the Lord proclaims that he who uses the sword shall perish by the sword?

And shall the son of peace, for whom it will be unfitting even to go to law, be engaged in a battle? And shall he who is not the avenger even of his own wrongs, administer chains and imprisonment and torture and executions?... The very act of transferring one's name from the camp of light to the camp of darkness is a transgression. Of course, the case is different if the faith comes subsequently to any who are already occupied in military service, as with those whom John admitted to baptism, and with the most believing centurions whom Christ approves and whom Peter instructs; all the same, when faith has been accepted and sealed, either the service must be left at once, as has been done by many, or else recourse must be had to all sorts of quibbling, so that nothing may be committed against God.... Do leaves make up the laurel of triumph — or do corpses? Is it decorated with ribbons or tombs? Is it besmeared with ointments, or with the tears of wives and mothers — perhaps of some even who are Christians — for Christ is among the barbarians as well? (*On the Garland* 11-12)

How shall the Christian wage war, no, how shall he even be a soldier in peacetime, without the sword which the Lord has taken away? For although soldiers had come to John and received the form of their rule, although even a centurion had believed, the Lord afterwards in disarming Peter ungirded every soldier. (*On Idolatry* 19)

Who shall produce truth, gentleness and justice with the sword, and not their contrary, deceit, harshness and injustice, which are the proper business of battles? (*Against Marcion* 3, 14)

(viii) Cyprian, a controversial bishop of Carthage from 248-58, was a follower of Tertullian. He too was an unequivocal pacifist.

The whole world is wet with mutual blood; and murder, which in the case of an individual is admitted to be a crime, is called a virtue when it is committed communally. Impunity is claimed for the wicked deeds, not on the plea that they are guiltless, but because cruelty is perpetrated on a grand scale. (*Letter* 1, 6)

We have not in such a way given our name to warfare that we ought only to think about peace, and draw back from and refuse war [a deliberate paradox, but he is speaking of martyrdom, as he goes on to show] when in this very warfare the Lord walked first — the Teacher of humility and endurance, and suffering — so that what he taught to be done, he first of all did, and what he exhorts to suffer, he himself first suffered for us. (56, 3)

God wished iron to be used for the cultivation of the earth, and therefore it should not be used to take human life. (*On the Dress of Virgins* 11)

Adultery, deceit and the taking of life are mortal sins..., after partaking of the eucharist the hand is not stained with blood and with the sword. (*On the Value of Patience* 14)

(ix) Mincuius Felix may belong to the second or third century. His work *Octavius* is one of the most attractive of early Christian writings. In it he states, rather as Athenagoras does: "It is not right for us even to see or hear of a man being killed" (30, 6).

(x) A number of anonymous writings of the period confirm the general picture. Typical is a speech of unknown authorship, attributed to Justin, which says "Be instructed by the divine Word and learn about the incorruptible King, and recognize his heroes, who never inflict slaughter on peoples."

(xi) Arnobius was another of the Latin Christian writers, who was converted from paganism and may at one time have been an Epicurean (who were in their own way also pacifist). His *Arguments Against the Gentiles* was accepted as evidence of the sincerity of his conversion.

(xii) Finally we come to the last of the great Christian writers before Constantine, and one of the most eloquent of all, Lactantius. Three quotations will here suffice. The third shows the nature of the Christian refusal of war; the others show something of the positive commitment which went along with it.

Someone will say here: "What therefore, or where, or of what sort is piety?" Assuredly it is among those who are ignorant of war, who keep concord with all, who are friends even to their enemies, who love all men as their brothers, who know how to restrain their anger, and to soothe all madness of mind by quiet control. (5, 10, 10)

Why should the just man wage war, and mix himself up in other people's passions — he in whose mind dwells perpetual peace with men? Is it likely that he who regards it as wrong, not only to inflict slaughter himself, but even to be present with those who inflict it and to look on, will take pleasure in human blood? (5, 18, 13)

When God prohibits killing, he not only forbids us to commit brigandage, which is not allowed even by the public laws, but he

warns us not to do even those things which are regarded as legal
among men. And so it will not be lawful for a just man to serve as a
soldier — for justice itself is his military service — nor to accuse
anyone of a capital offense, because it makes no difference whether
you kill with a sword or with a word, since killing itself is forbidden.
And so, in this commandment of God, no exception at all ought to
be made to the rule that it is always wrong to kill a man, whom God
has wished to be a sacrosanct creature. (6, 20, 15)

(b) The only discordant voice to break this hymn of peace is Julianus
Africanus. He hardly counts. He was seemingly a soldier before his
"conversion" (which did not run very deep). His miscellany entitled
Belts includes much obscenity, much sexual license as well as glory in
destruction. This apart, the nearest to any alternative voice is that
something approaching the later doctrine of the just war is found in
Tertullian and Origen. Both of them allow a relative justification of
violent acts for good motives in pre-Christian days or among
non-Christians. Gandhi later took a similar position. He preferred a
man who was not a committed *satyagrahi* to resist tyranny by violence
rather than to side with tyranny or to be indifferent to it. We have
already seen Tertullian and Origen's repudiation of bloodshed on the
part of the Christian. They are in fact not authorizing Christians to take
part in just wars; we have seen that the witness of the Christian writers
does not permit the Christian to be associated with the taking of life
"even justly." They are in fact turning the argument back on to the
pagans and saying "We who are Christians may not take part in war at
all. You who are not Christians had better be true to your own highest
standards and see that if you fight wars you fight only just ones." Later
Augustine applies the doctrine of the just war to the Christian, or
nominally Christian, state, but in so doing he rejects the central
traditions of the church in the first three centuries. The main evidence
is in the letters. Thus Augustine oddly defends the military profession
on the grounds that John the Baptist does not condemn it, and justifies
wars declared in a spirit of goodwill, in defense of the Christian faith, to
enable the defeated enemy to enjoy a peaceable commonwealth of
religion and justice (*Letters* 138, 14-15) . He commends those who fight
with peace as their aim, while adding that it is better to seek peace
through peace than through war (*Letters* 229, 2) . He distinguishes
among murder for selfish ends, judicial execution, and regrettable
necessity as in self-defense and war (*Letters* 153, 17) . Elsewhere he
rejects killing in self-defense but accepts it in defense of others or in

defense of the state (*Letters* 47, 5). It seems a long way from those who said that a Christian might not watch a man being killed, even justly, let alone kill him. It seems a very, very long way from the New Testament.

c) On the other hand, from A.D. 173 there were a certain number of Christians in the army. Before that we know of none except Cornelius and the jailer at Philippi, and we know nothing of their subsequent careers. In other words for nearly 150 years there is no evidence of Christian soldiers, in itself an eloquent testimony to the normal attitude. In the early 170s there is a curious story which shows a number of Christians in at least one legion. The twelfth legion, campaigning in central Europe, were suffering from water-shortage and in desperate straits. They knelt to pray: there was a clap of thunder and torrential rain. Christian apologists attribute the miracle confidently to the prayers of Christians in the legion. The record is in Eusebius's *History of the Church* (5, 5). The legion had been previously stationed in Cappadocia, and no doubt some of the troops were converted. At the beginning of the fourth century the emperors Diocletian and Galerius took the decision to purge the army of Christians. This suggests that though there were Christians in the army there were not very many in number; no commander can afford to eliminate a large number of his troops. From all this we can draw the following conclusions.

(i) Before 150 there were next to no Christians in the army. By the beginning of the third century Tertullian speaks of Christian soldiers, but up to 300 the number was small. The fourth century is the turning-point. At the beginning Diocletian purges the army of Christians, at the end Theodosius purges the army of pagans.

Let us take a simple parallel. Gandhi was unquestionably a pacifist. If we found that no follower of Gandhi was to be found in the army before the year 2100 and very few before the year 2250 we might think his pacifism of quite extraordinary power. If there was a change between 2250 and 2350 we should attribute it, rather sadly, to a falling away from a basic commitment.

(ii) No Christian would think of joining the army. Tertullian discusses the possibility to reject it (*On Idolatry* 19); he calls it a transfer from the camp of light to the camp of darkness (*On the Garland* 11); it is apostasy. The witness of Christian writing during this period is, as we have seen, explicit. In addition a work called *The Canons of Hippolytus*, which in its present form dates to about A.D. 500, but which contains earlier material, says explicitly "No Christian should go and become a soldier, unless a commander, who has a sword, compels him; let him not draw any guilt of bloodshed upon himself." It is unlikely that this is a new injunction in the fifth century; it is much more likely that it is a survival from the second or third century. It rejects voluntary military service, and enjoins the Christian conscript to refuse to take life. Similarly in a church order from Egypt statute 29 reads "A catechumen or believer who wishes to become a soldier shall be rejected, because it is far from God." It is the criticism brought by pagans against Christians that by their abstention from military service they were endangering the empire. So with Celsus in about 178 in the attack which Origen combated. It is interesting to find the same criticism levelled at the Christians in the fifth century by Volusianus. Even with the weight of state authority, nominally Christian, against it, pacifism remained strong (Augustine *Letters* 136; 138).

(iii) The problem lay when a soldier was converted. The solution was a compromise. In fact over much of the second century there must have been many soldiers in the Roman army who did not see battle. This was the immeasurable majesty of the peace of Rome; a wider area of the globe enjoyed a longer period of untroubled peace than at any time in the history of man either before or since. Many of the soldiers were engaged on peaceable and constructive building operations. It was hard to lay certain death upon a man who might not be called to kill. So the church did not demand that their converts leave the army, but they did not accord them full church membership until they did, rather as some churches in Africa have refused to accord full membership to regular members of their congregation unless they renounce polygamy. The evidence for this is to be found in church orders from Egypt and Syria, dating in their present form from the fourth century but clearly going back earlier. For example from Egypt statute 28 reads "They shall not receive into the church one of the emperor's soldiers. If they have received him he shall refuse to kill if commanded to do so. If he does not refrain he shall be rejected." From Syria we have a document entitled *The Testament of Our Lord*. In it we read: "But if soldiers wish to be baptized to the Lord, let them cease from military service or from the position of authority, or else let them not be accepted."

(iv) The tensions at the end of the third century saw Christians contracting out of the army and suffering martyrdom in consequence. We have some of their statements at their trials. Tarachus said "Because I was a Christian I have now chosen to be a civilian." Marcellus said "I threw down my arms; it was not seemly that a Christian man, who renders military service to the Lord Christ, should render it by earthly injuries." Maximilian said "I cannot serve as a solder; I cannot do evil; I am a Christian." We also have an epitaph erected by Pope Damasus over two martyrs Nereus and Achilleus.

> They had signed up for soldiery, undertaking cruel
> duties. Together they watched their overlord's commands,
> ready to do his bidding at the spur of fear.
> A miracle of faith! All at once they laid aside their madness,
> they turned, they fled, they abandoned the general's godless camp,
> they threw down their shields, their helmets and blood-smeared
> swords,
> they rejoiced to acknowledge and bear along Christ's triumphs.
> Through Damasus believe the power of Christ's glory.

(v) It is sometimes said that the real factor which drove the Christians out of the army was the idolatry not the bloodshed. The evidence is against this. As we read the above passages we see that idolatry is little mentioned; it is the bloodshed which was foremost in the mind.

(d) The general attitude of Christians towards their social responsibilities at this period may be seen in an attractive letter, probably datable to somewhere in the middle of the second century. The recipient was named Diognetus: the author is unknown. "Christians are not marked off from the rest of mankind by nationality or language or tribal custom. They do not live in cities of their own. They do not use some unfamiliar dialect. They do not practice some demonstratively different way of life. This teaching of theirs was not invented by some intellectual or mental acrobatics. Some people advocate humanistic philosophy; not they. They live in cities in Greece and elsewhere, where each has happened to be. They follow the local practices in dress, food and their general way of life, and in so doing reveal the wonderful, astonishing (as all admit) constitution of their own citizenship. They live in their own homelands, but as tourists. They share in everything as citizens and suffer as foreigners. Every foreign country is a homeland to them and every homeland a foreign country. Like all men they marry and bring children into the world; unlike others, they do not leave those children to die. They practice free hospitality but not free love. They are in the world, but not worldly in their practice. Their days are spent on earth, their citizenship is in heaven. They obey the established laws, and in the quality of their private lives go far beyond what the laws lay down. They love all human beings, and all human beings persecute them. They are unrecognized, and suffer condemnation; they are put to death and find life. They are beggars and make many rich; they are in utter need, and are abundantly rich in everything. They are dishonored, and honored in their dishonor. They are maligned, and are justified. They are abused and offer blessing. They are insulted, and respond with courtesy. The do good and are punished as wrongdoers, and in receiving punishment they are glad because they are receiving life. The Jews declare war on them as foreigners, the Greeks persecute them; and those who hate them cannot state the reason for their hostility. In a word what the soul is in the body, that Christians are in the world" (5-6). In this splendid passage we must pause to identify a number of features.

(i) The thought is closely based on the New Testament, and especially on Paul's letters, to which there are a number of allusions (*Rom.* 8:12-13; 1 *Cor.* 4:12; 2 *Cor.* 6:9-10; 10:3; *Phil.* 3:18-20).

(ii) The key to the whole passage is the assertion, based on *Philippians* 3:20, that the Christian exercises his citizenship of heaven through his citizenship of this world.

(iii) The general pattern is clear, and we have already identified it in the New Testament. The Christians did not seek to escape from their involvement in society; this has been said too glibly by people who ought to know better. They obeyed the laws and followed the normal practices of society, sharing in everything as citizens. They went far beyond the practice enjoined by the laws and set a moral example far higher than that shown by the rest of society. But there were points where they had to say No, and they said it fearlessly; their higher allegiance was to God.

(iv) The sense of the commitment to a way of universal, uncompromising love and a way of suffering remains strong. The suffering is seen more as a way to the glory of the sufferer than as a way of changing the world. The commitment remains.

(e) The real change came with Constantine. The extent of the change can be exaggerated—no doubt there was compromise before and no doubt higher standards remained after—but this was the decisive moment. Constantine was a soldier, born of a family of soldiers. His family were by tradition sun-worshippers. The sun was the latest deity to be used in an attempt to bring religious unity to the diversity of the Roman Empire: his all-seeing eye promised the just surveillance of all the earth and his scorching power made him an acceptable god to soldiers. When Constantine was marching on Rome to attain supreme power he saw a cross of light superimposed on the sun, a rare but attested version of the "halo-phenomenon," and somehow the words came to him "Triumph in this." He put some form of the emblem on his banners — it was not dissimilar to the chi-ro, the first two letters of the name of Christ in Greek — and he did triumph. Constantine now became a syncretist. The sign was a Christian sign, delivered by his ancestral god the Sun, and the Sun and the Son became fused in his mind. He did not become a Christian — indeed he was baptized only on his deathbed. He continued to issue coins depicting the Sun and other pagan deities. But he gave privileges to Christians; it was fashionable to be a Christian, and many climbed on the bandwagon of the church, and the taste of power tended to corrupt. When Constantine built the new capital, the Christian city, which he wanted to call New Rome but others named Constantinople, Constantine's City, he set there his own statue wearing the rayed crown of the Sun made, as he believed, from the nails which crucified Christ. Constantine was not insincere, but his openness was confined within the limits of a ruthless and implacable ambition. Nothing we know of him as a person would make us think of Christ. His god was always the god of power, never the god of love. He is one of the great makers of history, and one of the least attractive of them. To Christianity he was an almost unmitigated disaster. James Douglass in his *The Non-Violent Cross* (p. 199) has written admirably 'When Constantine raised the cross above his troops, he raised before the Christian Church the same temptation which Satan had set before Christ on the mountain with the sight of all the kingdoms of the world. And the Christian Church — for understandable reasons and without the critical perspective of 1600 years — accepted Constantine's offer." The church might have done well to reflect on the words of the New Testament "Alas for you when all speak well of you" (*Lk.* 6:26). Persecution could not destroy the church's witness; worldly power went far towards doing so.

THE POLITICAL DIMENSIONS
OF JESUS'S MINISTRY

THE POLITICAL DIMENSIONS OF JESUS'S MINISTRY

Group and Individual

The Bible is about the story of Israel, and of the new Israel which is the church.

It is in general true of most societies until comparatively recent times that the basic unit of thought is not the individual but the group, the family (meaning not "dad, mum and the kids" but the total lineage or clan), the local community and the tribe or nation, and these last are likely to be viewed as extended families deriving from a common ancestor. It was the proud boast of the Jewish people to be "children of Abraham" (*Mt.* 3:9). This sense of "corporate personality" is important. Religion and morality are both affairs of the whole community. There is individualism, but it is always seen against the backcloth of incorporation. It can be seen in Jeremiah and Ezekiel, though Hempel has shown the importance of the individual in earlier periods too. But always against the backcloth, the organic unity of the social group. Yahweh is primarily the God of Israel and only secondarily the God of individual Israelites.

The complex interrelation between individual and group is seen in the practice of representing groups under the guise of individuals. A particularly clear example may be seen in *Daniel,* where "one like a man" (7:13) is explicitly identified with "the saints of the Most High" (7:18). Throughout the prophetic books the title "servant" alternates between the individual and the people. A particularly good example of the last is "My witnesses, says the Lord, are you, my servant" (*Is.* 43:10; NEB "servants" has no justification. Deutero-Isaiah constantly uses "servant" of Israel [e.g. 41:8; 42:19; 44:1; 44:21; 45:4; 48:20]). But in the Servant-songs the servant is at one point explicitly identified with Israel

> He said to me, "You are my servant,
>   Israel through whom I shall win glory" (49:3)

and at another point equally explicitly not so identified

> "he was cut off from the world of living men,
> stricken to the death for my people's transgression" (53:8).

We are not here concerned with the problem of identifying the servant. We note merely that we cannot escape the corporate involvement. Whether the servant is an individual, historic or hoped for, a remnant or creative minority, or the whole nation, the prophecies are about the whole nation and their destiny.

A second example of a rather different kind may be taken from Paul's letters. These are, as we should constantly remind ourselves, the oldest surviving documents of Christendom, older than the four gospels in their present form. Paul is aware of the grace of God to individuals in his grateful awareness of the grace of God on his own life. He does not forget individual men and women; the personal greetings at the end of his letters are one of the warmest parts of them. But his thought is in terms of the corporate nature of groups. His letters are directed to "the congregation of God's people at Corinth" (1 *Cor*. 1:2), to the Christian congregation of Galatia (*Gal*. 1:2), to "the congregation of Thessalonians" (1 *Thess*. 1:1). This is little enough of itself. But he plainly thinks of them as a unity. "There is one body and one Spirit, as there is also one hope held out in God's call to you; one Lord, one faith, one baptism; one God and Father of all, who is over all and through all and in all" (*Eph*. 4:4-6). "You are all one person in Christ Jesus" (*Gal*. 3:28). Where that corporate unity is broken the church has ceased to be the church. "Is Christ divided?" (1 *Cor*. 1:13 AV). When Paul speaks of the church as the body of Christ, as he does continually (e.g. 1 *Cor*. 12:12-27; *Eph*. 4:4-16; *Col*. 1:18), he is following the traditional practice of representing the group as an individual, and he carries on his metaphor to show that each individual finds his identity only within the group, as a limb of the body.

Not only so. When Paul views the great sweep of history, he thinks of the calling of the group, the nation. The Jewish people have their peculiar vocation; the Gentiles, or Greeks (Paul varies in his language), are invited to share in that vocation. Paul's language continues the personal metaphor, calling the two groups a natural-born son and an adopted child (e.g. *Gal*. 3:29). The Jews were entrusted with the oracles of God (*Rom*. 3:2). The Gentiles were strangers to the community of Israel (*Eph*. 2:12). But Christ Jesus has reconciled the two in a single body to God through the cross (*Eph*. 2:16), and the Gentiles have become fellow-citizens with God's people (*Eph*. 2:19). Paul's language is couched in corporate terms because in his thought God is concerned with "the Jews," "the Greeks," and not merely with individuals who happen to be Jews or Greeks.

In fact Paul was, in C.H. Dodd's words, in quest of the Divine

Commonwealth. The keyword is here *koinonia,* which is variously rendered fellowship, communion, contribution, distribution, partnership, sharing and other terms in such a way as to obscure the fact that it is a common thread running through the New Testament. The word comes in *Acts,* of the *common* life of the church (2:42), and of the *sharing* of material resources (4:32). Both passages are to be seen in the light of the immediately preceding gift of the Holy Spirit. Indeed the common life of the church is to be seen as a *sharing* of the Spirit (*Phil.* 2:1), a *fellowship* in the Holy Spirit (2 *Cor.* 13:14: the basic phrase is the same), and also (for the NEB translation is too limited) a *fellowship* created by the Holy Spirit. This *community* finds its very being in sharing the life of Christ in the *communion* service (1 *Cor.* 10:16-17). It finds its natural expression and outcome in *contributing* to the needs of God's people (*Rom.* 12:13), in a *common* fund (*Rom.* 15:26), in being ready to *share* (1 *Tim.* 6:19). And—above all—it means a *shared* suffering (*Rom.* 8:17; 2 *Cor.* 1:7; *Phil.* 3:10), shared with Christ, but shared also with one another. In sum Paul can count Philemon his partner in faith, one in fellowship with him. The corporate unity of the church is a valid part of Paul's witness. The very context in which Paul speaks of the Eucharist makes it clear that he is thinking of the church as the new and true Israel (1 *Cor.* 10 *passim*). Christ is like a single body (1 *Cor.* 12:12; *Eph.* 4:13). And the word we translate "church" (*ecclesia*) means a public assembly of citizens summoned by a herald, and was used in the Greek version of the Old Testament for the commonwealth of Israel.

The Political Witness of the Old Testament

The Old Testament is a political book. In *Exodus* 21-23 we have a code of laws, sometimes called "The Book of the Covenant." They are the laws for a people, and the end of the last chapter makes it clear that the "you" addressed is the whole Hebrew people. But if this is true of the Book of the Covenant it is true also of the ten commandments. We are used to thinking of these as ethical injunctions to individuals. They are not; they are the summary of a code of behavior for a nation, and the Jewish people do right to use the Deuteronomic introduction "Hear, O Israel" (*Deut.* 6:4). The code of *Deuteronomy,* whatever its date—and scholars seem more divided than ever on this—does seem to be an expanded and humanized edition of the Book of the Covenant; it too is a code for a nation.

Throughout the historical books religion and politics are inextricably interwoven. Individuals may of course show righteousness and unrighteousness, but their offenses are seen as corporate. Achan takes forbidden booty and Yahweh punishes Israel by defeat; the offense is discovered and Achan and all his family are punished (*Josh.* 7). Again Saul slaughtered the Gibeonites; Yahweh punishes Israel for this long after Saul's death, with a famine; David hands over for execution two of Saul's sons and four of his grandsons, and they are killed "before Yahweh" (2 *Sam.* 21). Personal offense leads to political disaster, and is requited upon the family group. Even when the principle is affirmed in *Deuteronomy* (24:16), *Jeremiah* (31:29-30) and *Ezekiel* (18:2) that the individual stands responsible for his own sin, we cannot escape the corporate and political element. *Deuteronomy*, *Jeremiah* and *Ezekiel* are all concerned with the regeneration of *Israel*, and Jeremiah is intimately concerned with what we should today call his government's foreign policy.

Indeed, the prophets are concerned with social and economic righteousness. Amos inveighs against the fraudulent exploiters of the poor who cry "When will the new moon be over so that we may sell corn? When will the sabbath be past so that we may open our wheat again, giving short measure in the bushel and taking overweight in the silver, tilting the scales fraudulently, and selling the dust of the wheat; that we may buy the poor for silver and the destitute for a pair of shoes" (8:4-6). Amos is a particularly strong mouthpiece for social justice, but he stands squarely in the central prophetic tradition

> Money-lenders strip my people bare,
> And usurers lord it over them.
> O my people! your guides lead you astray
> and confuse the path that you should take.

That is *Isaiah* (3:12)

> Go up and down the steets of Jerusalem
> and see for yourselves;
> search her wide squares:
> Can you find any man who acts justly,
> who seeks the truth,
> that I may forgive the city?

That is *Jeremiah* (5:1)

> Is not this what I require of you as a fast:
>> to loose the fetters of injustice,
>> to untie the knots of the yoke,
>> to snap every yoke,
> and set free those who have been crushed?

That comes from the last chapters of *Isaiah* (58:6). In 1942 during the war Sidney Dark published a compilation entitled *The Red Bible*. He had no difficulty in finding suitable passages. The approach is somewhat unfashionable today. Amos is not Karl Marx, though Karl Marx stands more directly in the line of descent from Amos than some Marxists and some Christians care to remember. Jesus was not Lenin. But the prophets are ineluctably political and Jesus is of their line. The Bible may not be a Marxist tract. But it is not a Freudian tract either. It is not merely concerned with the inner self; it is concerned with the health of society.

The Political Context of Jesus's Ministry

It is impossible for anyone in a tribal society to conceive a purely individualistic ethic. It is impossible not to think corporately. It is impossible that a Jewish rabbi of the period of Jesus should divorce the personal from the political. Even if we were to exempt Jesus from these limitations, his words could not have isolated *for his hearers* the personal from the social, corporate and political. It is a matter of the climate of thought, the presuppositions, the framework of speech. To eliminate politics from the New Testament is to eliminate historical texture from it; it is to eliminate reality from it.

Above all in the seething Palestine to which Jesus came. S.G.F. Brandon has his own peculiar theory about the nature of Jesus's political involvement, but in *Jesus and the Zealots* he has spelled out the political context of the ministry with a fine sense of history.

Let us remember. Jerusalem was destroyed in 586 and the inhabitants deported. Fifty years later Babylon fell to Persia and they were allowed to return. They continued subject to Persia for two centuries, then after Alexander's coming subject to Greek dynasties, the Seleucids of Antioch and the Ptolemies of Egypt. The extreme Hellenizing policy of Antiochus Epiphanes led to revolt, and the accidents of history led to nearly a century of quasi-independence under the Hasmoneans. The period of independence is important; it helped to perpetuate the ambition for an independence which seemed improbable but never impossible. The coming of Pompey in 63 B.C. was the effective end of independence, though it dragged on for a further quarter of a century in an even more attenuated form, as a corner of a Roman province: these years saw continually violent uprisings, by Alexander in 57, Aristobulus and Antigonus in 56, Alexander again in 55, Pitholaus in 52, Antigonus in 41, in the attempt to reassert full independence. In the end Herod the Idumaean, a hated foreigner, came out on top. After his death in 4 B.C. there followed a troubled three-quarters of a century, first of divided authority between Herod's three sons, then a generation of Roman procurators in Judaea, then a brief unity under Herod Agrippa, and another quarter of a century of procurators. Rome was in the background when she was not in the forefront. And all the time the seething, militant demand for independence. When Jesus was born there were still those who could remember Palestine before Pompey, many who could remember it before Herod.

There are notorious problems about the birth-narratives in the gospels. According to one strand in the story Jesus was born before the death of Herod in 4 B.C. According to another his birth was associated with the census of P. Sulpicius Quirinius in A.D. 6. Neither accords with the traditional *Annus Domini* which starts our era. But the association of the birth with the census is the mark of a tradition which saw clearly Jesus's political involvement. In A.D. 6 the Romans took over the direct administration of Judaea and Samaria. The census was associated with the takeover; it was to form the basis for the economic administration. The case against the *publicani,* the tax-collectors, was precisely that they shared in the colonial economic rule; it should be noticed that Jesus in associating the tax-collectors with sinners and prostitutes was making a highly charged political comment (*Mt.* 9:10; 18:17; 21:31). The Jewish patriots were aroused by the census, and an independence movement pledged to violent resistance formed under the leadership of one Judas of Galilee, who is described by Josephus as a "dangerous professor" (*Wars* 2, 433; cf. 2, 118-119; *Ant.* 18, 1-10). Josephus names the rebels "brigands" (the Greek left-wing guerrillas of the 1940s were given the same name) or *sicarii* or dagger-men; he does not use the term "Zealot" or "Cananaean," which appear in the gospels (*Mk.* 3:18; *Lk.* 6:15), and which Josephus applies to the Jewish leadership in the war of A.D. 66-70. Judas raided an arms-store at Sepphoris. His revolt was crushed by the Roman legions, and two thousand of the revolutionaries were crucified outside the town along the road. Nazareth is not far. If Jesus was born before Herod's death he was 10 at the time. He may well have seen the crosses in the distance. He can hardly fail to have been impressed by the events. It was surely from here that he caught the vision of the way of the cross. To link these events to the birth of Jesus is to suggest that Jesus had the right way to meet Roman tyranny, where Judas was wrong. Both led to cricifixion. For the followers of Judas it was a punishment for violence. For Jesus it was the same suffering, voluntarily and innocently undertaken. This first was destructive, the second redemptive.

We can only summarize briefly the events of the years that followed. Our records are faulty. Josephus is our major source, but some of his words are cryptic, and he omits disturbances which are attested in the gospels. The period after Judas's uprising seems to have been peaceable. Quirinius deposed the high priest Joazar, which is curious, as Joazar was following the policy of appeasement; it will be noted that the way of Jesus was neither violence nor appeasement. The reminder that Rome controlled the high priesthood must have been gall to Jewish patriots (Jos. *Ant.* 18, 26). Valerius Gratius, procurator for the decade from A.D. 15 to 26, actually deposed and appointed four high priests; his last appointment was Caiaphas. The natural effect was to alienate the patriotic extremists from the high priesthood. When full war came in 66 we find the high priest Ananus opposing the Zealots and being killed by them (Jos. *War* 4,173).

Pontius Pilate was procurator from A.D. 26 to 36. Philo describes him as "naturally inflexible and relentlessly obdurate"; he charges him with "acts of corruption, insults, rape, outrages on the people, arrogance, repeated murders of innocent victims and constant and most galling savagery" (*Embassy* 301). Pilate was a protege of Sejanus, a virulent anti-Semite, who was, for a period before his fall, all-powerful at Rome. Pilate, probably early in his period of office, marched his army up to Jerusalem and quartered them there for the winter, standards and all. To carry the imperial insignia into the Holy City was a grave and seemingly deliberate offense to the Jews, and previous procurators had avoided this. The episode as told by Josephus is fascinating and frustrating. Pilate returned to Caesarea. Josephus records no violence in Jerusalem, but a massive nonviolent "demo," a march from Jerusalem to Caesarea, sixty miles away, and an orderly demonstration there for six days, not giving way before threats of violence, constant till Pilate withdrew the standards (Jos. *Ant.* 18, 55-59). These events must have taken place a year or two at most before the beginning of Jesus's ministry. Did he take part in them? Probably not, but we do not know. Who led the nonviolent protest? We do not know. Did he, or his methods, influence Jesus? Possibly, but we do not know.

Another curious event is recorded by Philo. According to this story Pilate set up in Herod's old palace in Jerusalem some golden shields. These bore no offensive portraits or emblems, but were inscribed with a dedication to the emperor. A delegation of Jews waited upon him and asked him to remove them. He refused, and they pleaded with him not to cause a revolt or break the peace. They threatened to appeal to the emperor. This threat upset Pilate, and it is important to understand why. The appeal was made to the emperor, and the emperor wrote to Pilate ordering him to change his policy (Philo *Embassy* 299-305). This makes it virtually certain that these events took place after the fall of Sejanus, at a time when Tiberius was again concerning himself personally with government. Now at this period the *Seianiani*, Sejanus's appointees and supporters, were subject to a purge. Sejanus had been condemned for high treason and they were suspect. Any accusation, however unjustified, might stick. If these events were before the crucifixion — whose date unfortunately cannot be precisely fixed — the threat recorded by the most politically alert of the gospel-writers — the threat recorded by the most politically alert of the gospel-writers, "If you let this man go, you are no friend of Caesar" (*Jn.* 19:12), was deadly. One charge had been answered with severe rebuke; a second could be fatal.

A third clash concerned the building of an aqueduct for Jerusalem. This was part of Roman civilization, and those who have lived in Africa and seen women whose whole life consists in walking miles to the nearest source of water and bringing back a full bucket on their heads, will not underestimate its civilizing power. Nothing wrong, except that Pilate ordered the costs to be met from the Temple treasury. Reaction was violent. There was interference with the work and offensive behavior towards Pilate himself. Pilate avoided a head-on confrontation with his troops, but had armed agents in disguise moving among the crowd, and on a signal using clubs to beat them up and disperse them (Jos. *Ant.* 18, 60-62).

Other disturbances are a shadowy background to the gospels. There were the Galileans "whose blood Pilate had mixed with their sacrifices" (*Lk.* 13:1). We know nothing of this event, and interpretations can only be speculative, but the term "Galilean" seems to have been synonymous with "Zealot" (S.G.F. Brandon *Jesus and the*

Zealots p. 54, n. 2). It is likely that Pilate's action was a requital of violence with violence, and it certainly seems that Jesus in his answer repudiates the policy of the Zealots: we must remember that the word translated "repent" could be legitimately rendered "find another policy." There was an attempted uprising at some point in the period before the crucifixion (*Mk.* 15:7), in which Barabbas was captured, and, we may suppose, the "brigands" who were crucified with Jesus (*Mk.* 15:27). It is merely perverse of Brandon to associate this uprising with the Cleansing of the Temple, but it shows something of the atmosphere in which Jesus came to Jerusalem. It was impossible to be apolitical. This was an atmosphere in which "He who is not with me is against me" (*Mt.* 12:30), and "he who is not against us is on our side" (*Mk.* 9:40). There was no neutrality.

It is not necessary to follow out the further clashes of the forty years that followed, though we should note that the Romans who arrested Paul expected him to turn out a Zealot (*Acts* 21:38); we are concerned with the ministry of Jesus. But it is worth a moment to consider the Qumran community. Now that the tumult and the shouting have died we can see that the more extravagant interpretations of the Dead Sea Scrolls are without foundation. The scrolls add to our understanding of the history and religious life of the period. They do not turn it upside down or transform it in any radical way. The sect appears to have begun at Qumran towards the end of the second century B.C. and come to a violent end in about A.D. 68. There is a curious hiatus in the history from 37 B.C. to 4 B.C., caused, it seems, by an earthquake which drove the community from the site. We are not here concerned with all the teachings of the sect. We have a monastic community, seemingly, withdrawn from the world, and, we might suppose, aloof from politics, perhaps even withdrawn in order to be aloof from politics. But they looked for the coming of a Messiah, or rather two Messiahs, who would usher in the era of righteousness. The document called *The War of the Sons of Light and the Sons of Darkness* portrays an apocalyptic Armageddon in which Belial will fight on one side and Michael on the other. So far this might seem to denote a spiritual warfare. But the initial enemies are "the Kittians of Assyria" and "the Kittians of Egypt." These may be mere phrases for the traditional enemies of Israel and not to be taken seriously. But the Jews of the last centuries B.C. called their Greek overlords Kittians, and the obvious reference would seem to be the Seleucids and Ptolemies. The war preparations seem very literal, and the spiritual troops are instructed in Roman military discipline, with rectangular formation, scissors-formation, wedge-formation, three-line battle order, shield cover, trumpets, standards, war cry. cavalry, slingers and men armed with seven spears. This may all be allegorical, but it has a frighteningly literal ring. However that may be it is a simple fact that the Qumran buildings were sacked by the Romans in about A.D. 68; there are iron arrowheads, broken walls, burnt buildings recalling the assault. It is possible that the devoted community had already left and that the building was occupied by fanatical Zealots. It is also possible that the community itself thought that they were participating in a war against the sons of darkness. Even a withdrawn religious community was politically involved.

The Messianic Hope

What was the Messianic hope? Israel of old had been a theocracy, a single political and religious community. The disasters of 721 B.C. and 586 B.C. had broken the unity. The exiles in Babylon had had to learn to live a life dedicated to God in an alien political environment, and Jeremiah more than any other had shown the way towards this. But the comprehensive nature of Hebrew religion made impossible a divorce between sacred and secular. As T.W. Manson put it (*The Servant Messiah* p. 2), "The religious soul of Israel must find a body. Hence the Messianic hope, the hope of restoring on a higher level the unity of national life that had been broken at the Exile." In the apocalyptic dream the Messiah, the Anointed, was to be the deliverer, the liberator, God's vicegerent in the restored kingdom. The pattern of expectation varied somewhat, but we can identify some of the principal features.

There was a strong tradition that the Messiah would be a military leader. This appears in the Old Testament, where the Messiah will break the nations with a rod of iron (*Ps.* 2:9), and shatter the yoke which fetters Israel (*Is.* 9:4-5). It is especially strong in the literature of Jesus and just before. For example in 2 *Esdras* 12:31-33 the Messiah is the lion who is to destroy the Roman empire. In the tremendous seventeenth of *The Psalms of Solomon*, one of the most important of the Messianic visions, the Messiah will reduce the Gentiles under his yoke. So too in Philo (*Rewards and Punishments* 15; *Execrations* 9) the foreigners will be repelled by the arms of the righteous under the leadership of a military hero (cf. *Numb.* 24:7). Similar passages could be adduced from the *Sibylline Oracles* (3:652) and from *The Apocalypse of Baruch* (70:9; though the verse may be an interpolation). The most extreme example of the military Messiah is in 4 *Ezra* (9:22 ff; 12:34; 13:37 ff) where the Messiah is not merely conqueror of the Gentiles but a merciless one. The general tenor of thought is that though the

Messianic kingdom would be a peaceable kingdom, it would be imposed by force: there is a striking parallel with the Roman empire. This is clear not least in the number of Messianic pretenders who raised the standard of violent revolt (cf. *Acts* 5:35-39). The major passage to the contrary is the familiar one from *Zechariah* (9:9-10). It is significant that Jesus on his entry into Jerusalem chose to fulfill that strand of prophecy, significant too that except in *Revelation* (19:11-21) the New Testament never takes up the idea of the military Messiah—and there the warfare is spiritual.

The second major aspect of the Messianic hope is that the scattered tribes of Israel are to be reunited in a restored Jerusalem. The thought dates back to the earlier periods of exile. "On that day," cried Isaiah (11:11) "the Lord will make his power more glorious by recovering the remnant of his people, those who are still left, from Assyria and Egypt, from Pathros, from Cush and Elam, from Sh..nar, Mamath and the islands of the sea." And again (27:13)

> On that day
> a blast shall be blown on a great trumpet,
>   and those who are lost in Assyria
> and those dispersed in Egypt will come in
> and worship the Lord on the holy mountain, in Jerusalem.

In *The Psalms of Solomon* it is the Messiah himself who will restore Jerusalem (17:33). Philo too speaks of the restoration of the exiles: he was a traditionalist and it was part of the tradition. It is important to remember that Babylon, the conqueror of 586, became a name for Rome (*Rev.* 18:2); these thoughts were vividly present. The tradition varied as to the role of the Gentiles. The extension of the vision in Deutero-Isaiah was on the whole forgotten.

> it is too slight a task for you, as my servant,
> to restore the tribes of Jacob,
>   to bring back the descendants of Israel:
> I will make you a light to the nations,
> to be my salvation to earth's farthest bounds. (48:6)

Though 1 *Enoch*, a composite book, but including the work of a highly original writer, preserves the vision of the Messiah as the light of the Gentiles (48:4). This should not be forgotten in considering Jesus's attitude to his Messiahship, in view of his explicit identification of himself with the Servant. The gospel writer did well to record the song of Simeon, who glimpses in the coming of Jesus "a light that will be a revelation to the heathen" (*Lk.* 2:32). Philo, strongly Hellenized as he was, looked forward to the eventual submission of the nations, whether freely or from fear, and one of the *Sibylline Oracles* (3) has a similar thought. In general the Messianic hope was for a restored Israel: the Gentiles would be conquered and driven away. There was no thought that they might be redeemed.

In the light of this, Jesus's prophecies of the fall of Jerusalem and the destruction of the temple were deeply shocking. They were completely foreign to the Messianic role as conceived by his contemporaries. They were tantamount to saying that the Messianic kingdom would not be centered on Jerusalem. Jesus has a wider hope. It is just here that the (admittedly difficult) story of the Canaanite (Syro-Phoenician) woman who came to Jesus when he was travelling along the coast (itself a significant fact) is so important (*Mk.* 15:21-28). She addresses him by the Messianic title "Son of David" and asks him to heal her daughter. The disciples try to send her away. If Jesus's next words are taken at their face value, he would never have spoken them; he would simply have allowed his disciples to hustle her off. He says, "I was sent to the lost sheep of the house of Israel, and to them alone." This is the traditional Messianic function. The woman makes a quick and witty reply, and Jesus commends her faith and heals her daughter. It is the final outcome that matters. We must assume either that Jesus, who took on human limitations with his human body, had had a limited view of the Messiahship, and this was for him a moment of illumination, or that he had all along held the wider view and was testing the woman. His silence is significant: he keeps a similar silence when confronted with the woman taken in adultery (*Jn.* 8:6) ; it suggests a sympathy with the woman and a rebuke to her opponents. I shall suggest that Jesus saw, or came to see, the Messianic kingdom, not as a restoration of Israel centered on Jerusalem, but the establishment of a new Israel which knows no national boundaries.

The third aspect of the Messianic kingdom is that it offered social justice. Isaiah saw it as sustained with peace and righteousness (9:7) ;

he shall judge the poor with justice
and defend the humble in the land with equity (11:4).

So in *Psalm* 72

O God, endow the king with thy own justice,
    and give thy righteousness to a king's own son,
that he may judge the people rightly
    and deal out justice to the poor and suffering (72:1-2) .

May he have pity on the needy and the poor,
    deliver the poor from death;
    may he redeem them from oppression and violence
    and may their blood be precious in his eyes (72:13-14) .

So in the seventeenth of *The Psalms of Solomon* the keynotes of the
Messiah's reign are wisdom, righteousness and equity. Philo too looks
forward to material prosperity, long life, large families, physical health,
peace, and security from wild animals. Here too was something which
Jesus saw as central to his own ministry. So he went to the synagogue at
Nazareth and read the passage

The spirit of the Lord is upon me because he has anointed me;
he has sent me to announce good news to the poor,
to proclaim release for prisoners and recovery of sight for the
    blind;
to let the broken victims go free,
to proclaim the year of the Lord's favor (*Is.* 61:1-2) .

This last year refers to the Year of Jubilee, when the land was supposed
to be redistributed equitably (*Lev.* 25:8 ff) . Then Jesus said, "Today in
our very hearing this text has become true" (*Lk.* 4:21) .

In all this we see that the Messianic hope was political, and that
Jesus accepted it as such while reinterpreting it.

The Political Dimensions of Jesus's Ministry

Let us then look at some passages in which the political elements in
Jesus's ministry seem clear. In some instances we shall be going over the
same ground twice, but we need to see the passages in context.

At the very outset Jesus is tempted by the devil. Among those
temptations is the temptation to possess the kingdoms of the world on
condition of homage to the devil, "the Prince of this world." This can
hardly be anything other than the temptation to political power by the
worldly means of military conquest, and Jesus rejects it (*Mt.* 4:8-10;
Lk. 4:5-8) . Jesus asserts *in a political context* "You shall do homage to
the Lord your God and worship him alone."

His first proclamation was of the coming of the kingdom (*Mk.* 1 14-15). This was bound to excite expectancies couched in terms of the Messianic kingdom. Jesus meant something different from this. He meant something which would more easily be expressed as the reign sovereignty or power of God (e.g. *Mt.* 12:28): the word "kingdom" suggests to us a visible organization which Jesus's words do no necessarily imply. Yet Jesus was concerned with a new community, and when that new community appeared one of their early concerns wa economic sharing (*Acts* 4:32).

The expectation that Jesus might be the Messiah runs through the gospel story. It is strongest in *John*. In his pages John the Baptist refuse the title of Messiah for himself, implying that the one who should come would be the true Messiah (1:20). Andrew having encountered Jesu goes to Simon Peter with the words "We have found the Messiah" (1:41). The woman of Samaria asks "Could this be the Messiah?" (4:29). The people actually try to proclaim him king, but Jesus slip away from them (6:15). They are obviously discussing whether or no he is the Messiah (7:25-31), and some of them say openly that he i (7:40). "The Jews" (presumably the leaders rather than the people) ask him directly, but receive an indirect answer (10:24-30). And o course in the synoptic writers Simon Peter declares Jesus to be the Messiah, and Jesus does not disown the title, and in one version says tha Simon has had a divine revelation (*Mt.* 16:13-20; *Mk.* 8:27-30, *Lk* 9:18-22). Further the entry into Jerusalem is a Messianic entry. On the cross Jesus was taunted with being Messiah (*Mk.* 15:32). It is the character of the Messiah he expounds on the walk to Emmaus, "the man to liberate Israel" (*Lk.* 24:21; 24:26).

One exceptionally interesting suggestion in this connection ha been made by Hugh Montefiore in an article in *New Testament Studie* (8, 1961-62; 135-141). The episode of the feeding of the five thousand (*Mk.* 6:30-44) has always been something of a problem, not only in relation to the nature of the miracle. Five thousand is a large numbe for a casual crowd wandering in the wilderness, and Montefiore doe not hesitate to say that "five thousand men did not follow their leade into the wilderness without good cause. It is hard to see a sufficien reason other than they wished to initiate a revolt." He points out that in the Old Testament "sheep without a shepherd" is used of a leaderles army (e.g. 1 *K.* 22:17), and that the arrangements in a hundred row of fifty each suggest 'not so much catering convenience as a militar operation." John intensifies the suspicion that there may be more her than meets the eye: it is in association with this event that he records the

ttempt to make Jesus a king. Jesus evaded this. He dismissed the people
nd "resisted a deliberate attempt to make him into a political and
nilitary Messiah," says Montefiore. Military, yes, but political? Is it not
ossible that he was demonstrating a politics based on peace not war, a
olitics of sharing and mutual concern?

The possible Messiahship of Jesus naturally raised expectations
mong the Zealots, the movement of military resistance. It is not
urprising to find a Zealot named Simon among Jesus's close followers
Mk. 3:18), and it is possible that the strange name Iscariot (Mk.
:19) may be a transliteration of the Latin *sicarius*, or "dagger-man,"
hough other explanations (e.g. in the Codex Sinaiticus "man of
erioth") have been proposed. And what of Peter? He carried a sword
Jn. 18:10). His name Bar-Jona (Mt. 16:17) may not mean "son of
ohn" (Jn. 1:42; 21:15) but may be an Accadian word for terrorist, as
uggested by Eisler and Cullman. James and John, the sons of thunder
Mk. 3:17) also behave like men of violence (Mk. 10:37; Lk. 9:54).
imon certainly, and the others possibly, must have joined in the hope
f Jesus leading a national uprising. But it is clear on the evidence of the
ospels that Jesus rejected Zealot policy. No Zealot would have
umbered a collaborator, a tax collector, among his followers (Mk.
:15; Mt. 9:10; 10:3). No Zealot would have healed a Roman soldier
r commended a Roman soldier's faith (Mt. 8:5-13). No Zealot would
ave said "Love your enemies" in a context which refers explicitly to
omans (Mt. 5:38-48). One of the most interesting passages in the
New Testament in this connection is the so-called parable of the wicked
usbandman (Mk. 12:1-12). In its present form this seems to be an
laborate allegory with God as the owner, the Jews as the tenants, the
rophets as the servants and Jesus as the son, and this is no doubt what
he story was designed to say to the church when it eventually appeared
n the gospels. But the Jewish rabbis, of whom Jesus was an outstanding
xample, did not use allegory—a parable is not an allegory, for it is
esigned to make a single point, not to work through a detailed
arallel—and this makes us suspicious whether this can be the form in
hich Jesus spoke the words. A story of an absentee landlord whose
enants use violence to avoid exactions and thus bring a major
ampaign to violence upon their own heads might well be in origin a
arning against Zealot policies. All who take the sword die by the
word; revolutionary violence provokes counter-revolutionary violence.
t is just to say that not all scholars would accept this interpretation.
ut, although it is unwise to build much on the orders in which the
ospel-writers have put together the *pericopai* (cut-outs, detached

passages or episodes) which make up the gospels, it is interesting tha
the parable appears in close proximity to Jesus's answer to the questio
about tribute to Caesar. And no Zealot would admit that anything wa
due to Caesar.

In his account of the entry into Jerusalem Luke has som
important words: "When he came in sight of the city, he wept over
and said, 'If only you had known, on this great day, the way that leac
to peace! But no; it is hidden from your sight. For a time will com
upon you, when your enemies will set up siegeworks against you; the
will encircle you and hem you in at every point; they will bring you t
the ground, you and your children within your walls, and not leave on
stone standing on another, because you did not recognize God's momen
when it came.' " (*Lk*. 19:41-44). Many scholars think that this passag
is colored by the gospel writer's knowledge of the siege of Jerusalem b
Titus in A.D. 70. But the language is very general: anyone writing wit
hindsight could have put a far more striking and horrific prophecy int
Jesus's mouth. Cool political realism without any supernatural insigh
could have made the judgment of the outcome of the Zealots' policie
Matthew too records Jesus as agonizing over Jerusalem (*Mt*. 23:37)
though there is some uncertainty as to exactly what he is saying. Th
apocalyptic discourse also foretells the overthrow of the temple (e.g
Mk. 13:1-2), and not many now would suggest that *Mark* is later tha
A.D. 70. Be that as it may, Jesus or the church or both say clearly
"There is a choice—Jesus and peace or the Zealots and destruction."

The last point that we must have established—and here S.G.F
Brandon is quite right—is that Jesus was executed for a political offens
In *John* even the initial arrest is undertaken by the Romans (*Jn*. 18:23)
Crucifixion was a Roman punishment; Jewish execution was by stonin
(*Acts* 7:57; Jos. *Ant*. 20, 9, 1). In laying the cross upon his followe
(*Mk*. 8:34) Jesus was foreseeing that the way he was electing to trea
was a way which the Roman authorities would, or might, regard a
rebellious. "Jesus" says T.W. Manson (*The Sayings of Jesus* p. 131) "
aware of an irreconcilable hostility between the Kingdom for which h
stands and the Empire represented by Pontius Pilate." It is perhap
easier for us to understand this than it was for those of an earli
generation. We know that Albert Luthuli expected to be, and wa
subject to repressive counter-measures by the establishment as much a
Nelson Mandela, Martin Luther King as much as Stokely Carmichae
But this makes nonsense of the suggestion that Jesus was apolitical. N
one is executed for being apolitical. Jesus was profoundly and relevant
political. He was executed for being King of the Jews (*Mk*. 15:2

15:18; 15:26). Gamaliel put him in the same category as Judas and Theudas (*Acts* 5:36-37). The curious story of Barabbas raises acute historical problems; since we have no other record of the unlikely practice of releasing a prisoner at the festival, and the name "Son of the Father" and the fact that some manuscripts as *Matthew* 27:16-17 call him Jesus Barabbas suggests that there is some kind of doublet of Jesus here. But the story reinforces the element of choice. Barabbas was a violent insurrectionist (*Mk.* 15:7; *Jn.* 18:40). It is the contrast between the man of violence and the man of nonviolent love, both arrested for political activity dangerous to the *status quo*. Jesus was and is "the man to liberate Israel" (*Lk.* 24:21) and all who are oppressed.

Jesus's Messiahship is different. There is a call to the people. We can here pick out five points which he advocates. First, he calls to national repentance (*Mk.* 1:15: the call to repent is in the plural). Second, he called for social justice, for community and commonwealth, for mutual concern and sharing. So far so good. Any Messiah might speak the same language. But, third, his Messiahship is one of peace, not war. Peace is both a means and an end. This is most clear in the entry into Jerusalem, fulfilling not the military prophecies but the peaceable prophecy of Zechariah. In *Luke* the crowds actually raise the cry of peace (*Lk.* 19:38) and Jesus contrasts his way with the way of the Zealots. In *John* the contrast again appears. "These [i.e. any who come before me] were all thieves and robbers." This cannot refer to the prophets. It refers to the Zealots. They led their deluded followers like sheep to the slaughter; Jesus is the true shepherd who lays down his life for the sheep. (*Jn.* 10:8; 10:11) This is the issue between Jesus called Messiah and Jesus called Bar-Abbas (*Mt.* 27:16-17: the issue is there whatever the right reading). Fourth, Jesus associates the Messiah with the Suffering Servant and issues a summons to suffering. He invites his disciples to be a suffering community; I do not doubt that he would have wished Israel to be that suffering community, but saw that neither the appeasers nor the Zealots would take that path. Finally, there is some indication that Jesus's answer to the nationalist rejection of Rome and the Romans was an extension of the grace of the gospel to Rome and the Romans (Greeks and other non-Jewish people).

This last point must be argued further. Consider the passage which Matthew places at the outset, immediately after the temptation:

"When he heard that John had been arrested, Jesus withdrew to Galilee; and leaving Nazareth he went and settled at Capernaum on the Sea of Galilee, in the district of Zebulun and Naphtali. This was to fulfill the passage in the prophet Isaiah which tells of 'the land of

Zebulun, the land of Naphtali, the Way of the Sea, the land beyond
Jordan, heathen Galilee,' and says:

> 'The people that lived in darkness saw a great light;
> light dawned on the dwellers in the land of death's dark shadow.'

From that day Jesus began to proclaim the message: 'The kingdom of
Heaven is upon you' " (Mt. 4:12-17). According to this version his first
preaching is to the Greek area and to Heathen Galilee, not just to the
Jews.

Now consider Jesus's assertion that the only sign that wicked
generation would receive would be the sign of Jonah (Mt. 12:39; 16:4;
Lk. 11:29). Matthew in one passage interprets this as meaning that
Jonah's incarceration in the big fish and subsequent release is a type of
Jesus's death and resurrection. But Luke is surely right in seeing that
Jonah was called to preach to Nineveh, and Nineveh was a Gentile city,
the capital of the brutal conquering military Assyrians, who stood to an
earlier generation of Israelites exactly as the Romans stood to the Jews of
Jesus's time.

Consider the parable of the mustard seed (Mt. 13:31-32; Mk.
4:30-32; Lk. 13:18-19). This has often been taken to be a parable
referring to the contrast between the seemingly small scale of Jesus's
ministry and the great proliferation of the kingdom to come. But Luke
does not mention the smallness of the seed. In the Old Testament the
spreading tree is used as the image of an empire with the birds and
animals in the shade standing for the subject peoples (Ezek. 31:39;
Dan. 4:10-12) and it is hard not to think that Jesus is referring to these
passages. The point is the same as in the parable of the feast: "From
east and west people will come, from north and south, for the feast in
the kingdom of God" (Lk. 13:29). From east and west, from north and
south, the birds flock to the shade of the tree. The outcasts of Israel and
the Gentiles alike share in the new order.

Consider further the implications of the song of Simeon (Lk.
2:29-32), of Jesus's encounter with the Roman centurion (Mt. 8:5-13),
of his embracing the Roman enemies within the community of love
(Mt. 5:38-48), of his preaching round the Greek area of the Decapolis
(Mt. 4:25; Mk. 5:20; 7:31), of his conversation with the Samaritan
woman at Sychar (Jn. 4:4-42) which ends with the assertion that Jesus is
the Savior of the world, of the bringing of the grace of healing to a
Samaritan leper who responds where others do not (Lk. 17:16), of the
implication of using a Samaritan as the example of loving behavior (Lk.

0:29-37), of the contact with the Greeks and Jesus's words *in that context* "In truth, in very truth I tell you, a grain of wheat remains a solitary grain unless it falls into the ground and dies; but if it dies, it bears a rich harvest" implying the spread of the kingdom among the Gentiles through the power released by his death (*Jn.* 12:20-33), of the Canaanite woman frm the coast who received the scraps from the Israelite table (*Mt.* 15:21-28), of the fact that at the crucifixion it was a man from Africa who carried the cross and who evidently became a Christian as a result since his sons were well-known in the church (*Mk.* 15:21) and that a Roman centurion at the moment of Jesus's death saw through his bodily frailty to his divine power (*Mk.* 15:39).

In other words Jesus offered an alternative policy to the policy of the Zealots. Part of this lay in his certainty that whereas violence breeds violence, suffering undertaken freely out of love is the channel of God's redemptive power. Part of it might be expressed with hindsight as the conversion of the Romans from within the Roman empire. But the two went together. Jesus did not acquiesce in Rome and all her works, or he would not have been crucified. To pay Caesar what is due to Caesar is to acknowledge some obligation to the imperial conqueror, but to couple this with paying God what is due to God is severely to circumscribe that obligation (*Mk.* 12:17). So the early church went out to make *all nations* Jesus's disciples (*Mt.* 28:19). Paul was the great missionary to the Gentiles, but he was not the only one. Peter began (*Acts* 10), then drew back (*Gal.* 2:12), but was in Rome when he was crucified. Philip reached out to the Ethiopian (*Acts* 8:26-31). Tradition has it that Thomas went to India: why not? These men were not interested in military revolt against Rome: they were transforming Rome from within. But their commitment led them to clashes in which the authorities showed violence, and they met it with an unflinching courage. And the blood of Christians became seed.

This remains the answer to our latterday Zealots. Christ has a better way.

THE WAY OF CHRIST

THE WAY OF CHRIST

We must now try to take a more comprehensive view of the New Testament.

Love

The way proclaimed by the New Testament is summed up in the word "love." The noun was to all intents and purposes, as those great experts in words J.H. Moulton and George Milligan put it, "born within the bosom of revealed religion." The verb existed, with a strong tendency to mean "put up patiently with." A man who, using this word (*agapan*), said "I *love* my wife" would mean "I put up patiently with my wife." "To love," using this word does not mean "to be emotionally involved with" but rather "to accept" in the fullest sense of that word, "to seek the well-being of," no matter what the other person does or how he behaves. It is a word of the will not of the heart. Anders Nygren in his great study *Agape and Eros* has shown that *eros* is the love which seeks to possess, but *agape* is the love which seeks to give. The noun is found in the Septuagint, the Greek version of the Old Testament, with the meaning of sexual love. This apart, there are very few occurrences of it before the New Testament. It makes only three appearances in secular Greek, and in all the readings is highly suspect (*P. Par.* 49, 3; *P. Berol.* 9859; Phild. *Lib.* p. 520). But in the Septuagint it is also used of Love shown towards God and towards that Wisdom which is God's effluence (*Wisd.* 3:9; 6:18). It was no doubt this that suggested the Christian usage, but the Christian usage goes far beyond this. Even in the New Testament the verb is commoner than the noun. Christian love is not an abstraction, it is an activity with an object.

In the New Testament love is first and foremost the very nature of God. "God is love" (1 *Jn.* 4:8) is the great Christian affirmation. Paul links this love, which is in God and which is God, with peace, and calls him the God of love and peace, in the very moment when he is urging his correspondents to live in love and peace; their behavior is to take its spring in the nature and being of God (2 *Cor.* 13:11). This is right. One thing which the New Theology has done is to bring God close, to get rid of the three-tiered universe with heaven the upper story, earth the ground floor, and hell the basement, and to seek for God not outside but within. If God is in very truth the depth of our being, of all being, as Tillich and John Robinson have insisted, we shall find our true way of life in the very nature of God.

There are three important corollaries of the fundamental assertion that God is love. First, love cannot be defined, for to define is to place limits upon, and it is impossible to place limits upon God. Love can be apprehended but not comprehended. It can be exemplified but not exhausted. Secondly, because love is primarily the very being of God and only secondarily seen in his relations with men it is impossible for love to degenerate into any kind of legalism without ceasing to be love. The witness of the gospels and of the epistles is here consistent. In the gospels Jesus replaces the old covenant of the Mosaic law with the new covenant which Jeremiah foreshadowed (31:31-33), and in so doing takes men into the freedom of God; in the epistles Paul, who had struggled to find fulfillment in obedience to the law found it, in the free response of love to love. Thirdly, because love is God, because it is God's nature to love, love is not called out by any merit in the recipient. "Christ died for us *while we were yet sinners*, and that is God's own proof of his love towards us" (*Rom*. 5:8). It was not merit in the sheep which sent the shepherd out to find it.

When we come to the human response we find identified the directions in which love is expected to operate. First towards God. It is the first commandment (*Mt*. 22:37; *Lk*. 10:27). This stated, the gospels do not say very much about love towards God, though John stresses love towards Jesus (*Jn*. 14:15; 21:15-17). Paul (*Rom*. 8:28; 1 *Cor*. 2:9; 8:3), James (2:5) and John (1 *Jn*. 4:20-21) speak naturally of loving God. The reason why there is not more stress upon this is partly that it is taken for granted, and partly that you cannot really command a person to love God; it is a natural response or it is nothing (1 *Jn*. 4:19). It might seem nonsensical to speak of loving God, or seeking his well-being. Not so. In some paradoxical way God needs us, has chosen to need us.

> What will you do, God, when I die?
> When I, your brother, broken, lie?
> When I, your drink, go stale and dry?
> I am your garb, the trade you ply,
> you lose your meaning, losing me.
>
> Homeless without me, you will be
> robbed of your welcome, warm and sweet.

I am your sandals: your tired feet
will wander bare for want of me.

Your mighty cloak will fall away.
Your glance that on my cheek was laid
and pillowed warm, will seek, dismayed,
the comfort that I offered once —
to lie, as sunset colors fade
in the cold lap of alien stones.

What will you do, God? I am afraid.

There, captured with the intensity of a poet's vision, in language which most of us would not dare to use, is the thought — God needs me. Rilke is only saying what Teresa of Avila said: "Christ has no body now on earth but yours, no hands but yours, no feet but yours. Yours are the eyes through which Christ's compassion is to look out to the world. Yours are the feet with which he is to go about doing good. Yours are the hands with which he is to bless us now." If I see a child slip and fall in the path of a car, and I do not snatch that child out of the way, God does not reach down a hand from heaven to do so. That child is killed. God needs me to save that child's life. He needs us to put an end to war. This is what Jesus means in saying "If you love me you will obey my commands" (*Jn.* 14:15). This is why John insists that love of God is shown in love of the brother (1 *Jn.* 4:20-21).

So we pass from the love of God to the love of men, and we find that the New Testament identifies three relationships in which love is shown. The first is within the church. The new commandment which Jesus gives in the Upper Room to the disciples is that they are to love one another (*Jn.* 15:12), and many of the injunctions to love in the epistles are primarily within the context of the church (e.g. *Rom.* 12:10). This seems at first sight surprising, turning the church into a mutual admiration society. We feel this because we are tainted with the heresy of individualism. But very much of the Bible, and very much of life, is about corporate action, about community, about fellowship. Those who have experienced Christian fellowship know that it is perhaps the most joyful experience which life has to offer. They know its evangelical power; they know how people hungry for love have cried "How these Christians love one another!" and by coming in for fellowship have come to accept the cornerstone of that fellowship. They know that a Christian fellowship which merely looks inward is not a fellowship at all, and ceases to be attractive even to those within it. The Dead Sea is a lake which allows rivers to flow in and none to flow out, and noxious substances accumulate there till life perishes. It is so with men.

The second relationship of love is towards the neighbor (*Lk.* 10:27). There is no question who the neighbor is. He is Everyman. He is everyone we encounter. He is the person we rub up against in life, the person in the next house, at the next desk in the office, next to us in the shopping queue or the bus. Jesus sharpens the point by giving an illustration in which the act of neighborly love cuts across the boundaries of racial and tribal prejudice and depicting a member of a despised group giving practical help to a member of a privileged caste, an outcast to a Brahmin, a black African to an exponent of *apartheid*, a Jew to a Nazi. Love is comprehensive. It excludes no one.

The point is further sharpened by the third relationship in which love is specified. This is towards enemies: as we have seen, the word embraces both personal and political enemies (*Mt.* 5:44). Love is God's means of meeting and *in the long run* winning criminals and imperialists and aggressors.

Love is an action. It is curious that some twentieth-century theologians have tried to oust love from its position of ethical centrality for the Christian, and to replace it by justice, accusing their opponents of abstract theorizing and claiming for themselves a concrete commitment to practical ends. The truth is that the New Testament knows nothing of justice, which is a term borrowed from Roman legalism, and the word sometimes so translated means "doing right." Justice is the abstraction. Love denotes an active, practical, personal commitment, and to do right is to love, and to love is to do right. "The first thing," said Ignatius Loyola, "is that love ought to be placed in works rather than in words." "Love proves itself in actions," said Teresa of Lisieux. Pastor Andre Trocme preaching in Newcastle in English, cried, "Have love in your hearts. No, my friends, forgive me, I do not speak your language well. I do not know what the heart is except an organ for pumping blood around the body. Have love in your lives." When Jesus had told the story of the Good Samaritan he did not end with the word "That is who your neighbor is" or "That is what love means" but "Go and do as he did" (*Lk.* 10:37).

Love is God's answer to evil, which is to say that it is the only way in which evil can be overcome, in the fundamental nature and being of the world. Love is the way for the Christian in the world as it is. The New Testament is not saying "Wouldn't it be nice if we all loved one another!" This is totally to misconstrue the nature of love, which does not depend on the character of those to whom it is directed. Of course it would be nice if we all loved one another, and the fact that we do not make love more relevant not less, more urgent not less. Love is not enjoined upon us in Utopia. We do not turn the other cheek only when there is no one to strike the first or go the second mile only in a world in which there are no armies of occupation. This is the way in which the Christian is to meet the hoods and thugs and militarists of this world. Love is not sentimental. It does not pretend that evil men do not exist. It offers a way to deal with them.

Love is not a temporary or local expedient. Those who have tried to make of love an *Interimsethik*, a temporary way of life pending the Day of the Lord, or those others who have accepted its relevance to the agricultural society of first-century Palestine but not to the sophisticated complexities of our twentieth-century conurbations, can find no justification in the New Testament. The New Testament never bases love on the nature of this "interim" or the imminent expectations of the Day of the Lord, still less on the particular nature of Palestinian society at this period, but on the nature and being of God.

Love is concerned with groups as well as individuals. We have seen the inescapable interaction of these in Jewish thought, and have seen that we are wrong to read back our largely post-Renaissance preoccupation with individuals into Biblical times. It is just here that Reinhold Niebuhr was so wrong. Niebuhr was a formidable critic of pacifism in the late 1930s and 1940s. It is not commonly realized that Niebuhr stated with complete clarity that the teaching of Jesus was "an absolute and uncompromising ethic" and inescapably pacifist, and that his ethic of love "is drawn from, and relevant to, every moral experience." Niebuhr's contention was that "human collectives are less moral than the individuals which compose them"—hence his famous title *Moral Man and Immoral Society*—and that love is not applicable to group relations. This is what Dean Inge (not a pacifist) in the *Fall of Idols* called "that ruinous dualism of public and private ethics. . . which by openly proclaiming that the teaching of Christ has no reference to the conduct of States has made modern Europe a hell upon earth" (p. 179). Pope Benedict XV in 1920 in his encyclical *Pacem Dei Munus Pulcherrimum* wrote "The Gospel has not one law of charity for individuals and another for states and nations, for these are but collections of individuals." Love has to do with the relationship of Jews and Romans, of Judaea and Rome. Love has to do with the Son of Man, a title which, as we have seen, may properly be understood of the community of Jesus and the disciples. Love has to do with the corporate being of the Jerusalem of which Jesus shed tears. Love has to do with Jesus's understanding of his Messiahship and his leadership of his people, the kingdom as well as the king. Love has to do with the Israel of which the prophets spoke, and of whose vocation as a martyr-nation the greatest of them was not afraid to speak, and with the new Israel which is the church. Love has to do with Christ, and so has to do with the body of Christ, which is the church.

Love is concerned with means as well as with ends. "For nothing in the world, neither for love of any creature is evil to be done" said Thomas a Kempis. Love cannot use evil means to encompass a good end. "The end justifies the means" is a philosophical confusion, for if the means are baneful, though the aim may be justified, the result will not be. Gandhi once said (*Satyagraha in South Africa* p. 318) "We are merely the instruments of the Almighty Will and are therefore often ignorant of what helps us forward and what acts as an impediment. We must thus rest satisfied with a knowledge only of the means, and if these are pure, we can fearlessly leave the end to take care of itself." So too Bishop Butler at Vatican Two: "Let us indeed show all sympathy for statesmen in their immense difficulties; let us gratefully acknowledge their good intentions. But let us add a word of reminder that good ends do not justify immoral means; nor do they justify even a conditional intention of meeting immoral attack with immoral defense. *Our help is in the name of the Lord, who made heaven and earth.*" Throughout the New Testament it is constantly asserted that love suffers. The suffering of Jesus is the supreme example of the love which refuses to meet evil with evil, violence with violence, hate with hate. "There is no greater love than this, that a man should lay down his life for his friends" (*Jn.* 15:14) . "Christ died for us while we were yet sinners, and that is God's own proof of his love towards us" (*Rom.* 5:8) . "It was clearly fitting that God for whom and through whom all things exist should, in bringing many sons to glory, make the leader who delivers them perfect through sufferings" (*Hebr.* 2:10) . "My present bodily life is lived by faith in the Son of God, who loved me and gave himself up for me" (*Gal.* 2:20) . "Live in love as Christ loved you, and gave himself up on your behalf as an offering and sacrifice" (*Eph.* 5:2) . "Husbands, love your wives, as Christ also loved the church and gave himself up for it" (*Eph.* 2:25) . "It is by this we know what love is: That Christ laid down his life for us" (1 *Jn.* 3:16) . And it is continually assumed that the Christian who accepts for his own life Christ's way of love will expect to suffer.

It is right here to say something about one of the more significant movements of the second half of the twentieth century. Apparently the phrases "ethical existentialism," "situation ethics" and "the new morality" were all phrases coined or adapted by Pope Pius XII in the 1950s. He condemned the new morality, insofar as it involved "a tendency to subordinate the objective moral law to some kind of subjective judgment which the individual claims to be immediate and decisive," but not insofar as it involves "the exercise of a proper prudence in the application of Natural Law to particular cases." The main champion of situation ethics in English is the American Joseph Fletcher, in his book of that title, and we may be profoundly grateful for much that he says. His book is in large part a defense of the way of love. He sums up his thesis in six propositions.

Only one "thing" is intrinsically good; namely love: nothing else. (p. 57)

The ruling norm of Christian decision is love: nothing else. (p. 69)

Love and justice are the same, for justice is love distributed, nothing else. (p. 87)

Love wills the neighbor's good whether we like him or not. (p. 103)

Only the end justifies the means; nothing else. (p. 120)

Love's decisions are made situationally, not prescriptively. (p. 134)

Of these the first, second and fourth are clear New Testament teaching, and the third is in full accord with the New Testament in subordinating justice to love. The fifth is ambiguous: does "end" mean "aim" or "result"? It is not, I think, in accordance with the New Testament, where the means are themselves determined by love, by the quality of the life of the doer, by the indwelling Spirit, and all of which we shall speak in the third section of this chapter. The last is the point of controversy.

At first sight it is a breakthrough which enables us to return to the New Testament. To love God and to love one's neighbor—everything in the law and the prophets hangs on these two commandments (Mt. 22:40). Hence Augustine's "Love God—and do as you like." Love is not law, though James speaks of it as the sovereign law (2:8); it would lose its nature if it became law. There is a proper sense in which every person and every situation is unique.

To this, however, there are two qualifications. One is that I do not in fact take a fresh moral decision in every situation I face. I do make general moral decisions. I do not, for example, ask in relation to every woman I meet "Shall I commit adultery?" Fletcher recognizes this. He claims that situational ethics brings together three things: "its one and only law, agape (love)"; the "Sophia (wisdom) of the church and culture, containing many general rules' of more or less reliability"; and "the Kairos (moment of decision, the fullness of time) in which *the responsible self in the situation* decides whether the Sophia can serve love there or not." In a later book, *Storm over Ethics*, Fletcher summed up his position: "Moral principles were made for men, not men for moral principles. That is situation ethics in a nutshell." Admirable, or nearly so. For Fletcher's formulation is a shade ambiguous. He does not allow for the possibility that his *Sophia*, his general principles, may spring from a community based on love. They will still not be absolute; nothing is absolute except love itself. Love can be expressed in a commitment which extends through a series of acts as well as in individual acts. Fletcher's formulation is too elastic. The responsible self in fact takes a general decision based on love, and does not decide in each situation whether that decision serves love. We expect it to do so, but will be open to the possibility that it may not. The change is seemingly slight, but in fact all-important. Jesus did not expect men to break the Ten Commandments. His first question to the man who sought eternal life was whether he had kept them (*Mk.* 10:19). But he was open to the possibility that a man might have to hate his father and his brother (*Lk.* 14:26). Fletcher tells two true stories in which it might reasonably be maintained that love would lead to adultery (a woman in a Russian prison-camp who could not return to her husband and children in Berlin when they needed her unless she was pregnant) or the taking a life (the decision of the officer in charge when a man in a shipwreck jumped into and endangered a full boatload of women and children). Anyone would be unwise to say dogmatically what was right in either situation. But both are quite exceptional. They might happen to one person in a billion once in a lifetime. Fletcher tells them in such a way as to weaken the general sense that love will not lead to adultery, and that love will not participate in war: the last is particularly unfortunate, as the actual example really has very little to do with the Christian answer to war.

The other qualification is that Fletcher allows insufficiently for the factor of commitment. Some aspects of this were discussed by E.L Allen in his contribution to my *Studies in Christian Social Commitment*. The New Testament well understands the nature of such commitment. "No one who sets his hand to the plough and then keep looking back is fit for the kingdom of God" (*Lk.* 9:62). E.L. Allen takes two examples. The first is the commitment to be a prophet.

> Whenever I said, "I will call him to mind no more,
> nor speak his name again,"
> then his word was imprisoned in my body,
> like a fire blazing on my heart,
> and I was weary with holding it under,
> and could endure it no more. (*Jer.* 20:9)

The second is the commitment to one man or one woman in marriage, and it is "for richer for poorer, for better for worse." These (to borrow the language of Karl Jaspers) are commitments "out of which we will." They do not just lay another obligation on us. They change our whole way of life. Fletcher ignores this factor of commitment. In particular he ignores the nature of Christian commitment. John Vincent in his stimulating *Here I Stand* has said that to men morality is a highly secondary need to new discipleship (p. 45). Ultimately love must be identified in terms of the Christian way of life in Christ.

There are few who taking love seriously would not see it as finding expression in a commitment such as that in the basis of the British Fellowship of Reconciliation.

1.   That Love, as revealed and interpreted in the life and death of Jesus Christ, involves more than we have yet seen, that it is the only power by which evil can be overcome, and the only sufficient basis of human society.

2.   That, in order to establish a world order based on Love, it is incumbent upon those who believe in this principle to accept it fully, both for themselves and in relation to others, and to take the risks involved in doing so in a world which does not as yet accept it.

3.   That, therefore, as Christians, we are forbidden to wage war, and that our loyalty to our country, to humanity, to the Church Universal, and to Jesus Christ our Lord and Master, calls us instead to a life-service for the enthronement of Love in personal, social, commercial and national life.

4.   That the Power, Wisdom and Love of God stretch far beyond the limits of our present experience, and that He is ever waiting to break forth into human life in new and larger ways.

5.   That since God manifests Himself in the world through men

and women, we offer ourselves to Him for His redemptive purpose, to be used by Him in whatever way He may reveal to us.

The Cross

We come now to the Cross, and this, in Chesterton's characteristic pun, is the crux of the matter. One of Reinhold Niebuhr's other assertions against pacifism was that pacifists did not take the fact of sin seriously enough. He had encountered too many sentimentalists of the "Hitler-can't-be-as-black-as-he's-painted" variety, who were believers in extending the right hand of friendship and never came to terms with turning the other cheek. And of course he did right to reject such sentimentalism. There is evil in the world, and there are people whose lives are dominated by evil, though we dare not say that there are any beyond redemption, even in this world. "Pass no judgment and you will not be judged" (*Mt.* 7:1).

It is the New Testament witness that God's answer to evil *in this world* lies in the Cross. I stress the words "in this world." The crucifixion of Jesus is an incident of history, datable, if we had full information, to a precise year, day, hour. "Crucified *under Pontius Pilate*" is a key phrase in the creeds of the church. It reminds us that we are dealing with a faith which is concerned with our life in this world, that the Word *became flesh*.

And what became flesh was the Word. We encounter here something greater than the execution of Socrates, the assassination of Gandhi, the murder of John Kennedy or Martin Luther King. The great fact about the Cross is that it is an act of God. "God was in Christ reconciling the world to himself" (2 *Cor.* 5:19). I have quoted elsewhere those exquisitely ironical words from Richard Jefferies's *Bevis: The Story of a Boy*: "The Crucifixion hurt his feelings very much; the cruel nails, the unfeeling spear; he looked at the picture a long time, and then turned the page saying, If God had been there, he would not have let them do it." Jefferies had in mind the famous story of Clovis, military hero of the Franks, hearing about the crucifixion and saying, "If I and my Franks had been there, it would never have happened." The Franks—or their first-century equivalents—were not there precisely because Jesus chose that they should not be there; he renounced the military method of meeting evil. God on the contrary was there, suffering and dying. "Anyone who has seen me has seen the Father" (*Jn.* 14:9).

It is important to see what this means. God in his eternal nature is not and cannot be other than is seen in Jesus. This is what is meant by the seer of Patmos, if the older understanding of the verse if right, when he wrote of "the Lamb slain from the foundation of the world" (*Rev.* 13:8) ; it is an entirely possible rendering which the NEB does wrong to exclude. Suffering is engraved deep upon the fabric of the universe. There is a cross at the heart of God.

And it is important to see what this means. As we have seen, the effect of the new theology has been to bring God nearer. A God wholly transcendent would be as irrelevant as Aristotle's Unmoved Mover: in some of his writing the greatest theologian of the twentieth century, Karl Barth, seemed in danger of leading men into this error: the Father of Jesus is not "wholly other." (In passing we may note that Barth wrote in his monumental *Church Dogmatics* IV, p. 550, "According to the sense of the New Testament we cannot be pacifist in principle, only in practice. But we have to consider very closely whether, if we are called to discipleship, we can avoid being practical pacifists, or fail to be so." There are many roads to the same destination.) A God wholly immanent would be subject to our relativities. But the God who is the depth of our being is the God who shows us what we should be. When we speak of God we mean, in Eric Mascall's phrase, "He Who Is." We mean the origin of all purpose, the source of all value. The Chinese have a concept called the *Tao* or Way. This is the way in which the universe works, the pattern, the harmony, the balance, the only way the universe can work. We are not concerned here with the particular content which Chinese thinkers have given to the *Tao*. The point is that it is for us to find the *Tao*, and live by it. One of the earliest names of the Christian church was "The Way." And when the New Testament was translated into Chinese, the opening words of *John* were rendered "In the beginning was the *Tao*....So the *Tao* became flesh." In other words — if we would see the only way in which the world will work we must look at Jesus. In fact this is the way in which we can most readily give contemporary meaning to the ancient formula about Jesus being fully God and fully man. If God is the depth of our being, there is — must be — a point where the two affirmations come together.

The Cross reveals God. It reveals the truth about the world in which we live. It reveals the Way. It is the way for us. So Jesus says, "Anyone who wishes to be a follower of mine must leave self behind; he must take up his cross, and come with me" (*Mk.* 8:34; *Mt.* 16:24; *Lk.* 9:23) . We are to accept completely the way of God. "There must be no limit to your goodness, as your heavenly Father's goodness knows no bounds" (*Mt.* 5 : 48) . Jesus did not merely go to the Cross; he at the least left it open — surely in hope — for his disciples to go with him (*Mk.* 10 : 38; cf. 14 : 26) . We can readily understand the worldy-wise finding the way of the Cross folly. In rejecting it they are rejecting Christ. To those who have he'ard his call he — on the Cross — is the power of God and the wisdom of God (1 *Cor.* 1 : 24) . This is why Mahatma Gandhi said, "If you Christians rely on soldiers for your safety, you are denying your own doctrine of the Cross." Conrad Grebel, leader of the Swiss Brethren, declared of Christians that "they use neither worldly sword nor war, for among them killing is done away with altogether." Grebel was influenced by Erasmus, but his approach is from God's side not from man's. His approach is scriptural, but it is not based on the Sermon on the Mount which he never quotes in this context. It is based upon the call to the church to be a suffering church. It is based on the Cross. The Cross is not a preference of tyranny to war. It is God's answer to both.

Christians have been reluctant to respond to the center of the Christian faith. Richard Baxter saw it and in the appendix to his *Dying Thoughts* wrote, "Oh! little, too little, do many honest Christians think how much of their most excellent obedience consisteth in child-like, holy suffering." We mouth the catchphrases, "*Via crucis via lucis*" (The way of the cross is the way of light) and (with William Penn) "No Cross No Crown"; we do not live them. There is no more ironical moment than the moment in Armistice Sunday when the massed soldiers on church parade, the government and opposition of the day, and civic dignitaries, join in singing:

> Sufficient is thine arm alone,
> And our defense is sure.

Tom Lehrer, the Harvard humorist and mathematician, has a wry comment:

> The Lord's my Shepherd, says the psalm.
> But, just in case, we'd better get a bomb.

Bishop Butler's speech at the Vatican Council quoted earlier in this chapter, strikes here to the heart. When we say that the way of suffering love will not work, when we accept, whether as a first or last resort, the need for military measures, we are saying in other words that we do not believe in the way of Christ and do not trust the power of God. Contrast these words of Gandhi's (*The Law of Love* p. 79) : "Though I cannot claim to be a Christian in the sectarian sense, the example of Jesus's suffering is a factor in the composition of my undying faith in nonviolence which rules all my actions, worldly and temporal. . . .Jesus lived and died in vain if he did not teach us to regulate the whole of life by the eternal law of Love."

Some of Christ's followers have set the example of "the best way of all" (1 *Cor.* 12:31). Peter, who had tried to deter Jesus from suffering, who promised to stand by him and then would not himself face the moment of testing, came to the way of the Cross long before he was himself crucified. Stephen took that road, Paul trod it all his life. Francis of Assisi took it. So did George Fox. So, in our own day, have Danilo Dolci and Albert Luthuli and Martin Luther King, to name but three. But it is not a way for a few eccentrics. This is a comfortable doctrine for ecclesiastical statesmen who cannot refute the pacifists but seek to keep them in the church. It is the way which is laid upon *anyone* who wishes to be a follower of Jesus. It is laid upon the church.

And Good Friday is transmuted into Easter. Not necessarily in three days. The Black Panthers who rejected Martin Luther King's commitment to Christ's way of nonviolence were understandably but wrongly impatient for immediate results. It is important here to be both utterly committed and coolly realistic.

First, we can never evaluate in experience the full results of our choices. For one thing, in making one choice we do not make another, and we can never know what would have happened if we had done so: in simple illustration, we can never know what would have happened if we had married the other woman, the other man. For another, even if we could do so, we are often dealing with incommensurables. What would have happened if there had not been military resistance to Hitler? We cannot tell. But, putting it at its worst, there is no scale to weigh the death and devastation caused by the war, with the spread of communist regimes over half of Europe, against the effects of Nazi domination of Europe with the extermination of Jews and others. No pacifist in his senses would claim to *calculate* that the effect of war was worse than the effect of tyranny. But non-pacifists claim to have made the opposite calculation. On what grounds? This apart from the possibilities that redemptive suffering might transform the situation. For another thing, the results of our choices are literally infinite; they reverberate down the corridors of future time; they spread horizontally beyond our gaze. And this means that we never see even the full results of the actions we take. A trivial example. I spent a period teaching at a school, took a deal of trouble over my own form, and, in the sin of vanity, was somewhat put out when none of them came to say good-bye. I thought that I had failed: perhaps I had. Then a boy whom I never taught came to thank me for what I had done for him. We look for results in one direction, and they come in another. A great example. Consider the results of Jesus's ministry, his commitment to nonviolent love, and, in particular, his decision to set his face towards Jerusalem, as they appeared on Good Friday evening and on the following Saturday. Ultimately we cannot judge by results.

Secondly, however, we can make some partial judgments. It is a simple fact that nonviolent methods do not add to the sum of destruction. It is also a simple fact that violence tends to provoke counter-violence, as indeed the Black Panthers found; indeed it tends to escalate, as the sorry story of events in Nigeria in the second half of the 1960s may serve to remind us. We may not always see the creative effects of nonviolence. The destructive effects of violence are plain for all to see. And as the weapons of destruction mount in power it becomes more urgent to renounce violence and accept instead of the risk involved in violence the risks involved in nonviolent love. It is wise to remember that the small "tactical" atomic weapons available for field use are more destructive than the bombs dropped on Hiroshima and Nagasaki. We can today see that World War II was embryonic in World War I. More, George Kennan in his story of *Russia and the West under Lenin and Stalin* (p. 32) has said, "The Russian Revolution and the alienation of the Russian people from the Western community for decades to come were only a part of the staggering price paid by the Western people for their insistence on completing a military victory over Germany in 1917 and 1918." Let us pray that World War III, to the X-ray eye of the historian so plainly embryonic in World War II, does not come to birth.

Thirdly, at the last it is a matter not of judging results, but of commitment to a way of life. Many of those who went into the 1939-45 war on the British side did not go in because they calculated that they would win, but because they felt it right to resist the Nazis and could see no other way of resisting. According to the New Testament. God does show another way, the way of nonviolent love, the way of the Cross. It is on this way that the Christian pacifist takes his stand. He knows, although he cannot foresee the outcome, that because the way of the Cross is God's way, through it God's will shall be done, and the good will prevail. He says, with Martin Luther at Worms, "Here I stand; I cannot do otherwise."

But it does work. By God it works. Three examples out of many which might be taken. The first from the experience of George Fox. "Look not at your sufferings" he wrote in a letter "but at the power of God, and that will bring some good out in all your sufferings; and your imprisonments will reach to the prisoned, that the persecutor prisons in himself." " 'Here is gospel for thee'," said Fox once to a man who threatened him, " 'here is my hair and here is my cheek and here is my shoulders', and turned it to him . . . and the truth came so over him that he grew loving" (*Journal* 1911, ii 4). It did not always so happen of course, though it should be noticed that we are far beyond the "right-hand-of-friendship" sentimentalism, and that it is the willing acceptance of suffering which evokes the change. But it happened often enough for Fox to write, "And there was never any persecution that came but we saw it was for good, and we looked upon it to be good, as from God; and there was never any prisons or sufferings that I was in but still it was for the bringing multitudes more out of prison" (*Journal* 1911, ii 338). Indeed the total example of the Quakers, individually and corporately, is a standing example of the power of suffering love. We can see it in their initial encounters with persecution, in their relations with the Indians of North America, in the work of the Friends' Ambulance Unit in facing the same dangers as the soldiers to heal the wounds of war, in the experience of countless individuals and groups in the transformation of situations of ugly violence by steadfast nonviolence and readiness to suffer.

The second example comes from France during the 1939-45 war. At Le Chambon-sur-Lignon there was an ancient Huguenot community whose leaders, the pastor, the schoolmaster, the doctor and others, had taken the commitment to nonviolent Christian love, and carried the community with them. Under German occupation the community was engaged in smuggling Jews out of the country into Switzerland. The Gestapo raided them from time to time. On each occasion they were warned by an anonymous telephone call. The members of the Gestapo were received with more cups of tea than they could drink — but they did not find the Jews. A young member of the community acted foolishly and hotheadedly, and was arrested and taken to the military headquarters. From there he smuggled a letter out to his friend the doctor, asking for help. The doctor did not see what he could do, but felt bound to do it. Taking a companion and trusting to his doctor's pass he drove to the town where the military headquarters were situated, and asked to see the commandant. He was granted his interview, and explained to the military commandant what they stood for in Le

Chambon. They hated the things which the Germans were doing but continued in constant love toward the Germans. They tried to prevent evil, but they did not believe in violent means and were not members of the *maquis*; they tried instead to overcome evil by good. While he was speaking in this way there was some crime committed in the town—a bank robbery, I believe. The town gates were shut. All cars were investigated and it was observed that the doctor's car had only the doctor's pass and not a pass to enter the headquarters. The car was searched and under the passenger's seat was found a revolver, which the doctor's companion had brought without the doctor's knowledge and in defiance of the doctor's whole way of life. The doctor was arrested, and died in the gas-chambers.

This seems a strange story to tell as a triumph of the Cross. On the face of it it seems a quixotic waste of a valuable life, and so, in a sense, it was. But the power of the Cross was there. It might be that our knowledge of the story stopped at that point. It happened we know more. For in this area there came a time when the resistance got the upper hand, and the Germans were imprisoned and interned. Andre Trocme, the pastor of Le Chambon, in visiting the prison camp met the commandant. He found that the German soldier had been so deeply impressed by the witness of the doctor, by his words, and by his willingness to give his life for his friend, that when the Gestapo purposed to raze Le Chambon as they razed Lidice and some Belgian villages, he refused to allow them. "No!" he said. "I do not understand these people. But I have talked with them and I know that they do not hate us. They are not killers. They are not in the movement of violence. You shall not do this thing." So, through the doctor's acceptance of the Cross the lives of all the inhabitants of Le Chambon were spared. More, they were able to go on with the work of rescuing the Jews. *But it is only by accident that we know this*. We cannot always see how God's love enters a situation through the obedience of his people. We know that it does so.

The third example is the most telling of all. It is a classic example of the way of the Cross in group relations. I have already touched on it. Here it is more fully told.

The story begins with Columbus's discovery of America in the fifteenth century, and the opening up of the new continent to European explorers and exploiters. The first European contact with Brazil was in the year 1500, when the Portuguese commander Cabral landed there on his way to the Cape and India; but it was not until 1531 that any systematic attempt was made to settle there: and only in 1549 was a central government established. The settlements along the coast achieved some prosperity, but little headway was made inland. But all over the Americas the story of the relations between the European invaders and the aboriginal inhabitants is a grim and sordid business. In Brazil the Indian tribes, in particular the Chavantes, were more ferocious than most, and refused to succumb. In 1650 an expedition in search of gold and diamonds crossed the territory of the Chavantes. They regarded this as in infringement of their hunting rights, and set upon the expedition as it was crossing a river. There was fearful carnage, and the river is to this day called Rio das Mortes, the River of Death. This incident set the pattern of future relationships between the government of Brazil and the Indians, and except where peaceful contact was certain, the general policy was based on the premise that "the only good Indian is a dead Indian" and the injunction to "shoot at sight."

So matters stood until 1910. In that year a young soldier in his early thirties, Colonel (later General) Candido Rondon, took over responsibility for relations between the government and the Indian tribes. Rondon was a remarkable man, whose name is surely written in the Book of Life. He himself was of Indian descent, and his great contribution was his ability to see the situation from an Indian point of view. He had the quality which Collier calls "empathy," the capacity for putting himself in the other person's place, for understanding him, in the vivid metaphor which that word originally contains. This is the beginning of Christian love. "Let this mind be in you which was also in Christ Jesus, who being in the form of God did not think equality with God a thing to be snatched at, but emptied Himself, and took upon Him the form of a man."

For Rondon this meant beginning with the Indians as and where they were, and accepting from the first the values inherent in their customs and ways of life. Hitherto the assumption had always been that Brazil existed for the sake of the European culture which had asserted itself there — there was in fact a war of cultures, and that could end only with the conquest of one culture by the other. Rondon challenged this assumption. In 1910 he became the director of a new organ, the Indian Protective Service; its very name betokened the change of outlook. The new approach was signalized by the use of airplanes (then, be it remembered, a comparatively new invention: it was imaginative to use them) to fly low over villages of the fierce Chavantes and drop gifts for the villagers.

What was more remarkable, however, was his deliberate espousal of nonviolence. Rondon was a soldier. He had fought against Indians:

indeed most of his campaignings had been from western outposts. He had seen intimate friends killed at his side by Indians. He had himself been wounded twice in such battles. But, like Brigadier-General Crozier after him, he came to see that war was not the way. The Indian Protective Service specifically decreed that firearms were not to be used against Indians, *even in self defense*. His instructions to his men were, "Die if you need to; but kill, never."

One of Rondon's early responsibilities was to develop the telegraphic communications of Brazil. Before 1910 it had seemed impossible. Heavy garrisons were maintained in the outpost stations, and even they could not suffice to protect the lines. The jungle region was inhabited by wild tribes who had never experienced anything but terror at the white man's hand. Many of the tribes had become desperate in the struggle to survive at all. Rondon built the telegraph line, and while building it, converted these fugitive embattles tribes to friendliness as he went along. Garrisons were now withdrawn. Indians who had once chopped down telegraph poles now freely reported the incidence of fallen trees on the lines. Some of Rondon's men lost their lives. But not a single Indian life was taken, and the work was carried through.

Rondon's biggest test came with the Chavantes. He sent twenty-six men in to establish friendly contact. At their first reception six were murdered; a few days later the remaining twenty were annihilated in an ambush. Not one fired back in self-protection. There was a nationwide furor, but Rondon refused to move from his position and to be jockeyed into the reprisals which were demanded. He prepared the ground for a new attempt with skill and care, and then sent a second expedition under Vanique. This group was unmolested. The men spread around demonstrating their friendliness. Soon the signs of hostility began to decrease, and they were able to make effective contact. Then one day there came to the encampment four hundred Indian warriors, with spears blunted as a mark of friendship, to make peace with the "tribe of white Indians." Rondon's comment was characteristic: "This is the victory of patience, suffering and love."

The story of the Indian Protective Service is an unusually good example of the Christian way applied to corporate relationships. It is such facts which make clear that the dogmatic affirmation of some theologians that this is not possible is unrealistic speculation. It is strange that those Christians who are harnessed to some sort of doctrine of "the just war" are not prepared to examine more closely the possibilities of the way of Gandhi and Rondon as a technique. But in truth we may see in it something deeper, a genuine expression of Christian love, and in its story of conquest through death, of the way of the Cross.

The Christian's Life in Christ

We come now to the last and climactic aspect of the Christian life as the New Testament presents it. We have seen Christ as preacher. We have seen Christ as pattern. We now see Christ as power. In the deepest sense the Christian life is not obedience to a series of commands. That is there, and it is hard to see what the Christian who admits that the ethic of Christ is uncompromisingly pacifist but says that we are not called to follow it, makes of such words as "You are my friends, if you do what I command you" (*Jn*. 15:14). In the deepest sense the Christian life is not the following or imitation of Christ, as one of the best-loved books of Christian devotion terms it. That too is there. The command to follow was a command to total involvement not just to physical motion! Jesus expects his followers to share his commitment and his suffering. "A pupil does not rank above his teacher, or a servant above his master. The pupil should be content to share his teacher's lot, the servant to share his master's" (*Mt*. 10:24-25). So the Cross is laid upon all who wish to follow him (*Mk*. 8:34). So Paul can tell the Corinthians "Follow my example *as I follow Christ's*" (1 *Cor*. 11:1) and can write of "the way of life in Christ *which I follow*" (1 *Cor*. 4:17). In the deepest sense the Christian life is the life in Christ.

The central expression of this in the gospels is Jesus's discourse in the Upper Room on the night of his arrest, as recorded by John. "I am the vine, and you the branches. He who dwells in me, as I dwell in him, bears much fruit; for apart from me you can do nothing" (*Jn*. 15:5). In the same context Jesus promises that the Father will send them another to be their Advocate—one who is "called in" for support, as counsel, or witness, or expert—and who will be with them forever, the Spirit of Truth, or the Holy Spirit, who will dwell in them, and teach them all they need, and who cannot come until Jesus has gone (*Jn*. 14:15-18; 14:26; 15:26-27; 16:7; 16:13). Whether Jesus spoke these words in this form, whether we are reading a reflection back of the experience of the church, or whether there is something of both scarcely matters here. The experience of the church brought together the command "Dwell in me, as I in you" (*Jn*. 15:3) and the promise. To put it differently. When Jesus said, "I have a baptism to undergo, and what constraint I am under until the ordeal is over!" (*Lk*. 12:50) he seems to have meant that one body was not enough to change the world, and until he had passed through the baptism of death he was in the straitjacket of a single body, but once he had entered into new life his Spirit could enter all who would open their lives to him. Peter at Pentecost speaks of Jesus as receiving the Holy Spirit 'from the Father and making the gift of the Holy Spirit to all who turn to him (*Acts* 2:33-39).

The Acts of the Apostles has been called without extravagance the biography of the Holy Spirit. From Pentecost his actions dominate every page. He seizes dramatically those who receive him. The very buildings are shaken (*Acts* 4:31); the people cry out in ecstasy and speak in strange tongues (*Acts* 2:4). The Spirit gives courage (*Acts* 4:31). He is manifested in the quality of life of individuals (*Acts* 11:23). He shows himself in a new willingness for sharing, for *koinonia,* for community (*Acts* 4:31-32). He inspires the disciples with the words they shall speak (*Acts* 4:31). From him comes healing power: it is with Peter only after Pentecost (*Acts* 3:1-10). He enables Stephen to see the glory of God (*Acts* 7:55). He directs Philip to the Ethiopian eunuch (*Acts* 8:29), and after that to Azotus (*Acts* 8:39-40); he prevents Paul and Barnabas from entering the province of Asia or Bithynia, and implicitly sends them to Europe (*Acts* 6:6-10). He guides the counsels and corporate decisions of the church (*Acts* 15:28).

The same pattern runs through Paul's letters. The Holy Spirit dwells in the Christian (e.g. *Rom* 8:9; 1 *Cor.* 6:19; *Eph.* 2:28). He shows us hidden truths, guides our understanding, tells us what to say (1 *Cor.* 2:6-16). He overcomes our lower nature and guides our conduct. (*Rom.* 8:4). His harvest is "love, joy, peace, patience, kindness, goodness, fidelity, gentleness and self-control" (*Gal.* 5:22). He guides also the most practical decisions, such as whether a widow should remarry (1 *Cor.* 7:40). The Spirit is spoken of indifferently as the Spirit of God or the Spirit of Christ or the Spirit of the Lord (2 *Cor.* 3:17) or the Spirit of Jesus (*Acts* 16:8; *Phil.* 1:19), and the indwelling of the Spirit does not seem distinct from the indwelling of Christ. "But that is not how you live. You are on a spiritual level, if only God's Spirit dwells within you; and if a man does not possess the Spirit of Christ, he is no Christian. But if Christ is dwelling within you, then although the body is a dead thing because you sinned, yet the spirit is life itself because you have been justified. Moreover, if the Spirit of him who raised Jesus from the dead dwells within you, then the God who raised Christ Jesus from the dead will also give new life to your mortal bodies through his indwelling Spirit" (*Rom.* 8:9-11). Again "In the same way, only the Spirit of God knows what God is. This is the Spirit that we have received from God.... A man gifted with the Spirit can judge the worth of everything. . . . We . . . possess the mind of Christ" (1 *Cor.* 2:11-16) .

Paul expressed this in other terms by calling the life of the Christian time and time again — nearly two hundred times — "the life in Christ." Sometimes he speaks of Christ in the Christian. The two are reciprocal: "Dwell in me, as I in you" (*Jn.* 15:3). There is a magnificent passage to this effect in *Colossians*: "The secret is this: Christ in you, the hope of a glory to come. He it is whom we proclaim. We admonish everyone without distinction, we instruct everyone in all the ways of wisdom, so as to present each one of you as a mature member of Christ's body. To this end I am toiling strenuously with all the energy and power of Christ at work in me" (*Col.* 1:27-29) .

The Christian life is the life in Christ. It is "Christ in you." It is the indwelling of the Holy Spirit, the Spirit of God, the Spirit of Christ, the Spirit of Jesus. What does this mean in practical terms?

Some years ago I wrote a pamphlet with the title "Would Christ have pressed the button?" The button was the button which released the atomic bomb on Hiroshima. My non-pacifist friends were critical: they had to be, for the answer was so clearly "No!" The question, they said, is not "Would Christ have pressed the button?" — that is an unhistorical question, for there was no button to press, so we cannot know whether he would have done so or not. (Can we not?) The question, they said, is "Would Christ have me press the button?", and we cannot, they went on, answer that by reference to the very different historical situation in the New Testament. They underestimate the relevance of the original question. In Charles Sheldon's still moving novel *In His Steps* a group of church members, realizing that their religion is merely conventional, resolve to take no action for a year without asking "What would Christ do?" Of course we cannot always tell, but it is an evasion to suggest that we never know for sure what he would — or would not — do, as Sheldon shows. Sheldon sentimentalizes very little. He makes clear the cost of discipleship, in divided families, and unemployment, and abandoned ambitions. He also makes clear the new power which it would be faithless to doubt would flow from such a commitment. Still, in the end, the critics were right. The question was a wrong one. So was theirs. The right question, the Christian question, is "What will Christ do — in me?" And I know that he will have no part in war; he cannot do so and be true to his nature, to his very being. His way is the way of nonviolent, suffering love, and if I do not put my worldly wisdom as a barrier to shut him out, this is the way he will continue to take in me. For "Jesus Christ is the same, yesterday, today, and forever" (*Heb.* 13:8) .

When Niebuhr claims that the pacifist underestimates not only the sin of tyrants and aggressors, but his own sin, he is right. We must be humble about our shortcomings. We do fail in our commitment. But when he says that this should change the nature of our commitment he is wrong. We may fall short, but we dare not choose less than the highest we have seen. When he says that "the grace of God is shown in pardon rather than power, in mercy for persistent sinfulness rather than a power of righteousness which so heals the sinful heart that henceforth it is able to fulfill the law of love," he is either unduly limiting the word "grace" or he is untrue to the New Testament, where pardon and power are both present. If he says that we cannot by our lower nature live out the way of perfect love, he is right. If he says that the Spirit of God cannot take hold of our lives and make them instruments of his purposes, he does not really believe in a god who acts in this world. Niebuhr's incisive critique has challenged us all, and he has been strong in the pursuit of social justice, but in the last analysis he has offered not good news about God but bad news about men.

And when my non-pacifist friends say scornfully that I suggest that Christians are called to be "little Christs," what else is the New Testament about? What else is meant by the thought that the church is the body of Christ, and we are members of that body? (And does this not mean that we are called corporately to the Cross, to the witness of nonviolent love, which is valid for groups as for individuals? What else is meant by Paul's assertion "It is now my happiness to suffer for you. This is my way of helping to complete, in my poor flesh, the full tale of Christ's afflictions still to be endured" (*Col.* 1:24)? What else is meant by John's "even in this world we are as he is" (1 *Jn.* 4:17)? "Every Christian," said Angelus Silesius, "must be Christ himself." In the words of Teresa of Avila already quoted, "Christ has no body now on earth but yours, no hands but yours, no feet but yours. Yours are the eyes through which Christ's compassion is to look out to the world. Yours are the feet with which he is to go about doing good. Yours are the hands with which he is to bless us now." There is nothing here for us to boast about. The power is not ours, but Christ's. The glory is not ours, but God's.

Christ showed us a new way, a way of life, a way of changing the world. It was politically relevant. It was *in its own way* revolutionary. It was the way of love, the way of the Cross, the way of nonviolence, the way of Truth-force, Soul-force, Love-force. It is still the way. He seeks to fulfill it in us.

INDEX OF SCRIPTURAL PASSAGES

INDEX OF PROPER NAMES